JACQUES
SCHIFFRIN

JACQUES SCHIFFRIN

A PUBLISHER IN EXILE, FROM PLÉIADE TO PANTHEON

AMOS REICHMAN

FOREWORD BY

ROBERT O. PAXTON

TRANSLATED BY

SANDRA SMITH

Columbia University Press *New York*

COLUMBIA
UNIVERSITY
PRESS

Columbia University Press gratefully acknowledges the generous support for this book provided by a member of our Publisher's Circle.

Columbia University Press
Publishers Since 1893
New York   Chichester, West Sussex
cup.columbia.edu
Copyright © 2019 Sandra Smith

Library of Congress Cataloging-in-Publication Data
Names: Reichman, Amos, author. | Smith, Sandra, 1949- translator.
Title: Jacques Schiffrin : a publisher in exile, from Pléiade to Pantheon /
Amos Reichman ; foreword by Robert O. Paxton ; translated by Sandra Smith.
Description: New York : Columbia University Press, [2019] | Includes
bibliographical references and index.
Identifiers: LCCN 2018040028 (print) | LCCN 2018053083 (e-book) | ISBN
9780231548403 (e-book) | ISBN 9780231189583 (hardcover : alk. paper)
Subjects: LCSH: Schiffrin, Jacques. | Schiffrin, Jacques—Exile. | Publishers
and publishing—France—Biography. | Publishers and publishing—United
States—Biography. | Jewish publishers—Biography. | Gallimard
(Firm)—History—20th century. | Pantheon Books—History—20th century.
Classification: LCC Z305.S37 (e-book) | LCC Z305.S37 R45 2019 (print) |
DDC 070.5092 [B] —dc23
LC record available at https://lccn.loc.gov/2018040028

Columbia University Press books are printed on permanent
and durable acid-free paper.
Printed in the United States of America

Cover design: Julia Kushnirsky

In memory of André Schiffrin

why are we telling these stories?
what have we come here to find?
what have we come to ask for?
far away in time and space, this place
is a potential memory to us,
a likely autobiography.
our parents or grandparents might have
found themselves here
it was most often by chance that they either stayed
or didn't stay in Poland, or stopped,
on the way to Germany,
Austria, England or France.

Georges Perec, *Ellis Island*

CONTENTS

ACKNOWLEDGMENTS

This book would not have been possible without the kindness and generosity of the Schiffrin family.

I would like to particularly thank Leina and Anya Schiffrin, who ceaselessly and with rare kindness helped me in my research and bestowed their trust in me.

Leina Schiffrin welcomed me to her apartment and allowed me to consult the personal archives of André and Jacques Schiffrin in the very unusual circumstances of the recent death of her husband, André. She allowed me to carry out this research under conditions I will never forget.

Anya, thanks to her consideration and the numerous discussions we had, as well as allowing me to consult certain archives in her home, also played a significant role in the completion of this work. Many thanks to her and her husband, Joseph, for their support.

I would also like to thank Natalia Schiffrin for her interest in this work.

This book would not be the same without the expertise of Philip Leventhal. My warmest thanks for his attention, his detailed editing, and his enthusiasm. In addition, I thank Columbia University, where I was welcomed for a year, for allowing me to carry out my research.

Thanks to Sandra Smith, an exceptional translator, for her work and kindness. I would also like to thank Nicole Pope for having provided an initial English text.

I wish to thank Robert Paxton for the extremely invaluable advice he gave me.

For the information they passed on, mainly on the Schiffrin family's genealogy, Micheline Pelletier and Kira Sipek also provided precious assistance. I thank them both.

In the United States, I would also like to express my gratitude to Svetlana Alexeïeff-Rockwell, who invited me to spend a day at her home in Westport, Massachusetts, where we spoke of Jacques Schiffrin, who had played such an important role in her life. Svetlana died in 2015; I hope that this book might pay homage to her in some way. I would also like to thank Stuart Blazer from Westport, a friend of Svetlana's, who accompanied us that day.

In New York, I would also like to thank Vincent Debaene for his advice and Ariel Colonomos for his reassuring presence and consideration throughout the year I carried out my research at Columbia. On the other side of the Atlantic, in Paris, my gratitude to Emmanuelle Loyer, who advised me on my research and worked with me on seeing this book through.

Since history deals with the transmission of knowledge, I would also like to thank some of my professors, Daniel Henri, Philippe Masanet, and Vincent Lemire, who instilled in me the meaning and love of research.

Always, I thank my parents.

Finally, I would like to thank Bastien, Camille, Ella, Federico, Guillaume, Jean-François, Olivia, Oriane, Pauline D., Pauline S., Romain, Quentin, Samuel, Simon, Timothée, Vincent, and Vivian, who, whether in Paris or New York, were always with me.

FOREWORD

ROBERT O. PAXTON

The celebrated publisher Jacques Schiffrin made his way through the turmoil of the twentieth century with a mixture of success and suffering. A victim of war and racial prejudice, he endured exile twice. On two continents, first in Paris and then in New York, innovative publishing ventures brought him fame, though not wealth. At the end of World War II, ill with emphysema in New York, he could not reclaim the place he had lost in the Paris publishing world.

Growing up in a prosperous Jewish family in Imperial Russia, Schiffrin enjoyed economic security but faced discrimination. So, shortly before World War I, he left for Western Europe. After study in Switzerland and work in Italy with the art expert Bernard Berenson, he finally settled in Paris in the early 1920s. In France, homeland of the Declaration of the Rights of Man and of the Citizen, the first nation to grant full citizenship to Jews, Schiffrin flowered. Elegant, witty, and cultivated, he acquired a circle of interesting friends. In 1923, he founded the *Éditions de la Pléiade*, which published translations from Schiffrin's native Russian. He soon branched out into other classic works. In 1931, he had the idea of offering meticulous French-language editions of classic works in an elegant but affordable format: the *Bibliothèque de la Pléiade*.

Between 1931 and 1940, sixty-one volumes appeared in the *Bibliothèque de la Pléiade*. The format—leather covers, fine India paper with gilt edging, authoritative editing, convenient size—met with instant success. Schiffrin's choices were highly personal. They reveal him as a modernist, a cosmopolitan, and a lover of language with a taste for writers of marked individual character. This was not your conventional student reading list. Baudelaire was volume one in the *Bibliothèque de la Pléiade*, followed by the prose of Edgar Allen Poe. Other foreign authors among early *Pléiade* volumes included Shakespeare, Cervantes, Plutarch, Goethe, Tolstoy, and Plato. Racine was the first French classic author chosen. Lesser-known masterpieces like Choderlos de Laclos's *Les Liaisons dangereuses* were resurrected. André Gide was the first author published during his lifetime, in 1939. The *Bibliothèque de la Pléiade* contributed significantly to the prestige of French culture in the 1930s. What reader of French, in whatever part of the world, does not treasure a neat line of its volumes on their shelves?

World War II ended Schiffrin's French idyll. France was quickly defeated. (Schiffrin, a French citizen since 1937, had served in uniform.) Marshal Philippe Pétain, a hero of World War I, emerged to accept the armistice offered by Hitler and to head a new French government dedicated to purging the nation of ills that had allegedly caused defeat. Under the armistice, German armies occupied Paris, Northern France, and the Atlantic and Channel coasts. Pétain, from a temporary capital at Vichy, a spa town in the southern hills, governed the semi-autonomous Unoccupied Zone in the south.

On November 5, 1940, in German-occupied Paris, Gaston Gallimard, of whose publishing house the *Bibliothèque de la Pléiade* was now a part, dismissed Schiffrin from the enterprise he had created. Gallimard had bowed to Nazi instructions to remove Jews from positions of economic and intellectual influence.

Moving to the Unoccupied Zone offered no alternative. There the Vichy regime was proceeding, on its own and without direct German pressure, to remove Jews from public service, intellectual positions, and, eventually, business. Schiffrin had to leave his beloved France altogether in order to practice his profession. When he and his family boarded a ship in Marseille on May 15, 1941, dock workers jeered them.

So Jacques Schiffrin, his wife, Simone, and their six-year-old son, André, left for a second exile. Their trip to the New World was an ordeal. It was difficult enough to obtain all the necessary documents simultaneously: a French exit visa, an entry visa into the United States (the American government was notoriously unhelpful to European refugees in this period), and passage on a transatlantic ship. Even then, as happened to the Schiffrins, one could be turned back by the British blockade of Vichy French shipping. Once aboard, the passengers were crowded into insalubrious lower decks for maximum profit. The Schiffrins' miserable journey from Marseille to New York took three months.

Upon arrival in the United States, refugees from Hitler's war, even distinguished ones, often had to accept menial work. Simone kept the family afloat for a time by making accessories for women's clothing. Jacques helped out. But Schiffrin knew many European writers exiled in the United States. By 1943, he had found his footing in new publishing ventures. First, his own enterprise, Jacques Schiffrin & Co., published French authors like Gide in the United States. He then went into partnership with the German Jewish refugee publisher Kurt Wolff and his Pantheon Books. Pantheon became a fresh voice in the New York publishing world.

Schiffrin made a notable mark in a golden age of book publishing. In the first half of the twentieth century, with literacy nearly universal and without distractions such as television and the internet, books had become the essential medium of intellectual and cultural life. Only the cinema had comparable cultural heft, but the young medium of film complemented rather than competed with books. Several qualities allowed Schiffrin to excel among publishers: He was remarkably creative in identifying literary opportunities. He never compromised the taste or quality of his work. And he had an extensive range of friends among the major writers and intellectuals of his day.

Amos Reichman has combed through archives on both sides of the Atlantic to recover Schiffrin's correspondence with these friends, notably André Gide and Roger Martin du Gard. Schiffrin and Gide were particularly close; the older man offered essential financial and emotional help when the Schiffrins were stuck in Morocco on their way to New York in 1941. Schiffrin became Gide's publisher in the Western Hemisphere. Who else knew that Gide bought a blue DeSoto automobile with his U.S. dollar royalties from Pantheon in the late 1940s? Schiffrin shared his deepest feelings with his correspondents. His letters give this biography its attractive intimacy.

Schiffrin filled an important intellectual role in New York during and after the Second World War. He was a significant cultural bridge, not only with France but with Europe in general. But Schiffrin was never fully happy in the New World. Amos Reichman deals sensitively with the incurable sadness of exile, a pain that Jacques Schiffrin felt with particular force.

After the war, Schiffrin wanted to go back to Paris. It might have seemed self-evident that he would return to the direction of the *Bibliothèque de la Pléiade*. But *Pléiade* now belonged outright to Gallimard, thanks to German "Aryanization" orders.

Gaston Gallimard had promised to fulfill his contractual obligations to Schiffrin in his November 1940 letter of dismissal. But what were those obligations? Schiffrin had long been replaced as director of the series, and the French publisher does not seem to have explicitly invited him to resume the direction of the *Biblithèque de la Pléiade*.

In any event, Schiffrin's health made the trip impossible. A life-long smoker, Schiffrin was diagnosed with emphysema while serving in the French Army in 1939. His condition worsened in New York. By the end of the war, in 1945, he was too ill to travel. So he remained stranded in New York until his death at age fifty-eight on November 17, 1950.

Jacques Schiffrin's legacy as a publisher is immense. Both of his creations continue today, under different auspices. In France, the *Bibliothèque de la Pléiade* has become the arbiter of classic status. An author who receives a definitive *Pléiade* edition today has arrived. The Pantheon Press, continued later by André Schiffrin until the firm was bought out, enriched English-language publishing. Jacques Schiffrin led an exemplary twentieth-century life, with its share of brilliant achievement and personal pain.

JACQUES SCHIFFRIN

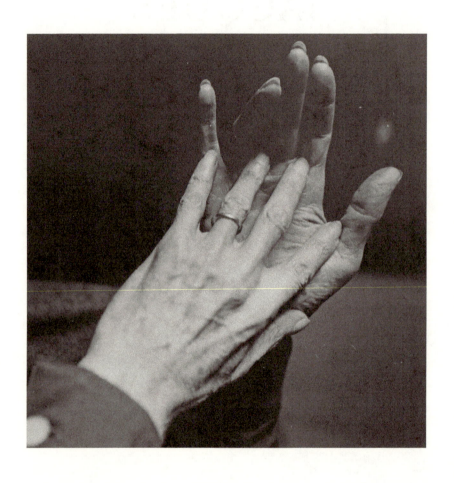

INTRODUCTION

It was around nine o'clock in the morning at the end of November; the ground was beginning to thaw. The train from Warsaw raced along at top speed toward St. Petersburg.

—Fyodor Dostoyevsky, *The Idiot*, 1869

On September 15, 1840, towards six o'clock in the morning, the Ville-de-Montereau *was about to leave; it spewed great clouds of smoke into the air opposite the Quai Saint-Bernard.*

—Gustave Flaubert, *L'Éducation sentimentale*, 1869

S o begin two of the most important novels of the nineteenth century. As Prince Myshkin heads toward St. Petersburg, Frédéric Moreau leaves Paris. The Great Russian Novel and the Great French Novel: two worlds that provided spiritual sustenance to Jacques Schiffrin, the founder of the *Éditions de la Pléiade*. In 1941, forced to flee with his wife and child into exile from France, where he had built his life and career, Jacques Schiffrin, too, would find himself on ships and trains: a ship from Marseille to Casablanca, a train from Casablanca to Tangiers, and finally, a ship from Tangiers to New York.

Jacques Schiffrin was born in Baku on March 28, 1892, and died in New York on November 17, 1950. His life story reads like a novel. But in the first half of the twentieth century, history seems to have overtaken fiction, leaving in its wake vast shifts in populations and virtually unimaginable transformations and irreversible tragedies, including the fate of Jacques Schiffrin. His life is closely linked to both the Russian Revolution and the Second World War, two major events that brought with them departures and arrivals. The theme of exile is thus at the heart of Jacques Schiffrin's life: first, his exile from the Russian Empire, which had become the Soviet Union, leaving the young Schiffrin no choice but to wander through Europe before settling in Paris in the 1920s; then, in 1941, again in exile, this time from France, which had become part German, part Vichy. Schiffrin, who was Jewish, had no choice but to flee, as quickly and as far away as possible.

Jacques Schiffrin's life thus encompasses both the catastrophes and hopes of the twentieth century. From Baku to New York via Paris, his life was influenced by two great events in history: the Russian Revolution and the Second World War, events that would be fundamental in determining the fate of this extraordinary publisher. Schiffrin belonged to a generation whose lives were determined by catastrophic moments in history. Yet Schiffrin knew how to grow stronger in the face of such terrible obstacles. He contributed to and was motivated by the spread of knowledge, and he introduced humanistic, classical culture to as many people as possible. While in exile, he built powerful bridges between countries and across oceans. The founder of the *Éditions de la Pléiade* in Paris, he helped introduce Russian culture to the French, while building a temple of classical French and Western literature that remains strong today. From New York, through his position at Pantheon Books, he helped pass the torch of European culture on to the New World. Thanks to him, some of the most important European writers and thinkers were published, discovered, and read in the United States. Through his work as a publisher, Schiffrin would become a mentor of the twentieth century, a guardian of classical culture, and an advocate for new voices.

Jacques Schiffrin's story begins in the Russian Empire, more precisely in Baku, the current capital of Azerbaijan. At the end of the nineteenth century, Baku was a key city in the Empire: "a city located at the border between the Russian Empire, the Ottoman Empire and Persia, Baku was the main port of Transcaucasia and the world capital of oil at the turn of the century."[1] It was a city where it was possible to make your fortune, and its oil held the promise of a prosperous future. But Baku was also a major asset at the crossroads of the geopolitical tensions that swept across European and Asian empires at the end of the nineteenth century, and this status contributed to the city's unique atmosphere. Thanks to its strategic location, it also attracted floods of immigrants.

In his autobiography, *A Political Education: Coming of Age in Paris and New York*, André Schiffrin, Jacques's son and a publisher himself, describes his father's childhood in Baku:

> My father, Jacques, had been born in Russia in 1892, beside the Caspian Sea in Baku, the oil-rich capital of Azerbaijan. His father had gone there to work as a longshoreman. Eventually, my grandfather had been struck by the fact that the Caspian surrounding the city was always aflame. Surely something could be done with the oil waste that was being dumped daily into the water? He met a young Swedish chemist, Alfred Nobel, who had been lured to Baku by the oil rush, and set about learning from him the basics of chemistry. He found that the waste could be turned into usable

petrochemicals, so my grandfather began approaching the oil pro-
ducers with offers to buy it. They were amazed at his stupidity but
agreed readily. Thus guaranteed a steady supply of inexpensive raw
materials, the Schiffrin petrochemical works was soon flourishing,
supplying tar and other products to much of Russia. . . . In sum,
my father grew up in very comfortable surroundings.[2]

In 1879, three of the Nobel brothers, Alfred, Emil, and Ludvig,
founded the Nobel Brothers Petroleum Company in Baku, and
it was with this company that Jacques Schiffrin's father, Saveli,
made his fortune.

Saveli Schiffrin was born around 1860, likely in Nijni
Novgorod,[3] a town approximately four hundred kilometers east
of Moscow, and, at the time, an important commercial center
within the Russian Empire. Saveli Schiffrin's parents were probably from Chernigov province, in current-day Ukraine. It is
likely that the Schiffrin family took advantage of the special laws
in Chernigov province that allowed Jewish populations from
the Russian Empire to live there; they then emigrated to Nijni
Novgorod, undoubtedly to profit from its vigorous economic
growth. But in the end, it was in Baku that Saveli Schiffrin
settled permanently, at the beginning of the 1890s, just before
Jacques was born.

At the age of twenty-four, Saveli married Fenya Litvinova,
a local woman from Moscow who had grown up on the outskirts of the Russian capital. Before arriving in Baku, Saveli and
Fenya Schiffrin had already had three children: Hélène, whom
they called Lyolene, Léon, and Eugénie. Jacques, whose name
was officially recorded as Yakov, was born in Baku on March 28,
1892. Two years later, Saveli and Fenya had another son, Simon,
who would eventually play an important role in the life of his
older brother Jacques.

When he was five or six years old, Jacques lost his mother, who died in childbirth. The baby, Boris, was stillborn.[4] Shortly afterward, Saveli followed Jewish custom and married Fenya's youngest sister, Elisabeth, and they had four children together. The Schiffrin family lived in relative comfort in the Bieli Gorod district, literally "the White City," an industrial suburb of Baku where Saveli's asphalt factory, the Kianda,[5] was located. In 1913, thanks to Saveli's financial success, the family moved to a large house in the center of Baku.

And so, Jacques Schiffrin grew up in Baku. A brilliant student, he passed his final exams in 1909, excelling in particular in French, German, Latin, and philosophy.[6] Shortly after moving into their large home in Baku, the Schiffrins continued climbing the social ladder by moving to St. Petersburg, the cultural and economic capital of the Russian Empire. However, Jacques did not go with them; he left Russia sometime between 1909, after finishing his final exams in Baku, and the beginning of the First World War. As André Schiffrin explains in his memoirs, his father initially traveled to Switzerland:

> The family later moved to St. Petersburg and, as the First World War approached, my father decided to go to Geneva to study law and, I assume, to escape the Czarist draft. Those Swiss years seem to have been very happy ones. He had more than enough money to live very comfortably and made many close friends, among them the Swiss psychologist Jean Piaget, as well as, I gather, a great many women. He cut a dashing figure, was a skilled skater, and led what seems to have been a carefree student's life. I know little more about this period; however, I am puzzled by some of its mementoes. For example, a Bible presented to my father by Rabindranath Tagore, the Indian philosopher; it has a long, very high-minded dedication by Tagore dated 1918. They must have been good friends, but I don't know how this came about.[7]

By studying law in pacifist Geneva during the First World War, Jacques Schiffrin was being educated in the heart of Europe, meeting well-known intellectuals like Rabindranath Tagore, who won the Nobel Prize in Literature in 1913 and whose work was translated into French the same year by André Gide. At this point, Schiffrin knew Gide, *le contemporain capital* ("the leading contemporary figure"), only by reputation. Ultimately, the two would become great friends.

In Switzerland, Schiffrin would come across some of the Russians in exile, people with whom he could discuss literature and politics. Between 1914 and 1917, Vladimir Ilyich Ulyanov, more commonly known as Lenin, was also living near Lake Geneva, dreaming of an ambitious revolution to bring down the Czarist regime and abolish private ownership of the means of production and distribution.

Ultimately, of course, Lenin succeeded and came to power in Russia by the end of 1917, and, in March 1918, he accepted harsh German peace terms, ending the war on the Eastern Front eight months before it ended elsewhere. But these developments put an end to any hopes the young Jacques Schiffrin might have had of returning to Russia. The government had nationalized the family business, making it impossible for him to go back to revolutionary Russia, where he wouldn't have had a penny and would have been forced to defend a regime he didn't support. According to André Schiffrin, his father left Geneva for Monte Carlo, where he made a fortune playing roulette.[8] Afterward, he spent time in Italy, probably toward the end of the 1910s, moving to Florence, where, according to his son,

[he] somehow got a job there as the secretary to Bernard Berenson. They worked together for several years, and as a result of this collaboration my father would later publish Berenson's *Italian*

Portraits of the Renaissance. While in Florence, he was also hired
by Peggy Guggenheim to teach her Russian.[9]

Jacques Schiffrin's European education continued in the heart of
the Renaissance, with one of the greatest living art historians of
the time, Bernard Berenson, a young Harvard graduate who had
been born in Lithuania, and alongside Peggy Guggenheim, a
young New Yorker who was already a sophisticated art collector.

Jacques Schiffrin's education was therefore complete: He was
nearly thirty years old, had mastered Russian, French, and Italian, and had knowledge of German and Latin. He had already
lived in three countries: Imperial Russia, Switzerland, and Italy.
France would be his fourth. He had been born into a world that
had already disappeared: the world of the czars. Then, in 1919 or
1920, Jacques lost his father, who died of a heart attack.[10]

Jacques Schiffrin arrived in Paris soon after the death of his
father. There his personal life and career truly took off. After working with Bernard Berenson, he was employed by Henri Piazza, a
publisher of art books specializing in expensive illustrated editions.
Piazza took Jacques under his wing, allowing him to help with
various projects. Working alongside Piazza, the young Russian
improved his skills, especially in the techniques of book publishing. Drawing on his new competence and what remained of his
family fortune, in 1922, Jacques Schiffrin would launch the most
important project of his life: He founded a new publishing house
that would influence literary history, the *Éditions de la Pléiade.*

The *Pléiade.* The name resonates far beyond the world of literary history. The *Pléiade* collection is truly part of French heritage.
It could, in fact, be considered a *lieu de mémoire,* as described by
Pierre Nora: an item of historical significance, an object that
runs through the collective imagination and is in some part
a basis of our common identity. In France, a country where

literature occupies a special, almost religious, place, the *Pléiade* is considered as highly as the Panthéon. Emmanuel Macron, the president of France elected in 2017, understood this fact: In the background of his official photograph, taken in the Élysée Palace, are three books: *Mémoires de guerre* by Charles de Gaulle (open on Macron's desk), *The Red and the Black* by Stendhal, and *The Fruits of the Earth* by André Gide. All are *Pléiade* editions.

The *Pléiade* founded by Jacques Schiffrin includes the classics of world literature. Since it was established, only 224 authors[11] have been published in this prestigious collection. The great majority of these authors were no longer alive when they made their "entrance" into the *Pléiade*, from Plato and Cervantes to Rimbaud and Proust. Their publication in the *Pléiade* resembles a kind of accolade[12]: These authors have been brought into the temple of great literature. Only eighteen authors have been published in the *Pléiade* in their lifetimes, including Milan Kundera, Claude Lévi-Strauss, and Eugène Ionesco, as well as Jacques Schiffrin's great friends André Gide and Roger Martin du Gard. Little by little, the *Pléiade* became a "cultural monument,"[13] with the role of defining what is considered great literature, both from the past and the present.

Why did Jacques Schiffrin choose to give his collection the name *Pléiade*? According to his son André, it was his father's Russian origins that were the deciding factor: "The name did not come from either Greek mythology or from the French Renaissance,[14] but from a group of classical Russian poets" in Pushkin's circle whom Jacques Schiffrin admired. Alice Kaplan and Philippe Roussin, however, offer a different explanation, but one also linked to the Russian origins of the collection's founder: "Schiffrin's *Pléiade* was from the Russian *pléiada*, and according to oral tradition at Gallimard, it meant 'to package up': The books would be beautifully produced."[15]

When he founded the *Pléiade*, Schiffrin's idea was to make the greatest literary works in the world available to as many people as possible in an accessible format. Schiffrin wished to make quality more generally available by targeting the *Pléiade* collection at a broad readership rather than producing books only for the elite. As André Schiffrin noted, "the *Pléiade* Proust would be less expensive to buy than all the volumes in the regular editions, for example."[16]

In addition to making works of great literary quality widely accessible, Jacques Schiffrin also wished to make his *Pléiade* editions physically beautiful. The books were and continue to be printed on paper used for bibles and are wonderfully illustrated, in particular by Russian painters living in Paris in exile. In 1933, an advertisement in one of the leading French literary reviews, the *Nouvelle Revue Française*, described the typography used in the *Pléiade* editions in detail:

> The *Pléiade Editions* have been produced according to entirely new principles: elegant, easy-to-handle, small books (11 × 17.5 cm), with a soft leather cover, we provide an enormous amount of text. . . . The font we chose, a magnificent Garamond, is perfectly legible. . . . Even though there are a great number of pages, the thickness of the volumes is normal, around 2 cm. The use of very expensive India paper, fine, opaque and sturdy, allowed us to attain the desired result.[17]

From its inception, the *Pléiade* represented a type of literary modernity, which coincided with the launch of its first collections of paperback books. Jacques Schiffrin's collection met the needs and expectations of a new generation, living in smaller spaces and always on the go. Books had to be smaller and easy to carry. As Alice Kaplan and Philippe Roussin emphasize, "The

Pléiade was not 'junk reading,' but train reading. The advantage of the bible paper (actually obtained from cigarette paper manufacturers!) was that you could fit many, many pages of print in a volume small enough to take in a suitcase."[18]

The idea for publications suitable for these new uses was discussed in an interview given by Jacques Schiffrin to the magazine *Toute l'édition* in 1933, in which he looked back on the early days of the *Pléiade*:

> You mustn't give me more credit than was my due in this business. I've traveled a lot: it was the English and the Germans who made me think I should publish the works they found so successful in France. However, as always when it is a matter of doing something innovative, I had to overcome a great many obstacles. French readers, I was told, do not like bound books. Today, I don't think anyone would reproach me. I wanted to create something useful and practical, you see. I took into account that the size of modern apartments requires fitting the maximum number of things into the smallest of spaces. And since I also loved books, I was determined that they be as beautiful as possible. That's all there is to it.[19]

As Kaplan and Roussin point out, in the apartments of the modern world, the books published in *Pléiade* editions would always have a special place: "If you walk into the library of anyone who reads in French, chances are strong that the *Pléiade*s will not be mixed with the other books but displayed together on the shortest shelves, their leather bindings touching one another."[20]

If the physical form of the works published contributes to the fame of the collection, it is also the choice of works that distinguishes the *Pléiade*. Schiffrin surrounded himself with specialists. In particular, he worked with his friend, the translator and essayist Boris de Schloezer. Born in the Russian Empire in 1881, Schloezer emigrated to France after the 1917 revolution. In the 1920s, Schiffrin published Russian titles in the *Pléiade* in a collection called *Classical Russian Authors*, which he translated with close friends. This included works by Dostoyevsky, Tolstoy, Pushkin, Gogol, and others.[21] The first book, published in 1923, was a translation by Jacques Schiffrin, Boris de Schloezer, and André Gide of Pushkin's *The Queen of Spades*, with illustrations by the Russian-born Vassili Choukhaeff. As mentioned earlier, Schiffrin's Russian friends often illustrated these works; for example, Alexandre Alexeïeff, a Russian illustrator born in Kazan in 1901 who emigrated to France at the beginning of the 1920s and whom Jacques Schiffrin would meet again a few years later in New York, created a hundred lithographs for *The Brothers Karamazov*, published in the *Pléiade* in 1929.

And so it was that Jacques Schiffrin, born in Baku at the end of the nineteenth century, contributed to the publication of treasures of Russian literature in France during the interwar period. He was a vigorous promoter, and through his efforts, the greatest Russian authors crossed borders and made a name for themselves in Paris. While paying homage to his country of origin by bringing the "Russian soul" to life, he participated in making France international, a country open to the world, which, with Schiffrin, would turn toward new horizons.

The initial years of this literary adventure, and the financial associations among Schiffrin and other Russian emigrants who made the early days of the *Pléiade* possible, were described in detail by Pierre Assouline, a historian of French literature:

> [Jacques Schiffrin] first found premises in Montparnasse, at the corner of the Boulevard Raspail and the Rue Huyghens. Then, with 280,000 francs as funding, he founded a limited-liability

company with the help of three other Russians living in Paris: his brother Simon, a future film producer (*Port of Shadows*, etc.), his brother-in-law, Joseph Pouterman (born in Kichinev in 1890) who had already published several beautiful illustrated books by Julien Green, among others, and Alexandre Halpern (born in 1879 in Petrograd), a very close friend and a naturalized Englishman who would become one of Winston Churchill's political advisors when he was a Minister and Member of Parliament. The company was formed on November 16, 1929, as the *Éditions de la Pléiade*.[22]

Forming the *Éditions de la Pléiade* as a limited-liability company gave legal status to the publishing house, even though volumes had been appearing since 1923.

In 1931, with the publication of Charles Baudelaire's *Œuvres poétiques*, Schiffrin launched a new collection: the *Bibliothèque de la Pléiade*. The catalog quickly grew after Baudelaire, with Racine,[23] Voltaire, and Stendhal joining the list of published authors in the *Pléiade*. The fifth author to appear in the new *Bibliothèque de la Pléiade* was neither Russian nor French: It was the American writer Edgar Allan Poe, translated by Baudelaire. Jacques Schiffrin was no longer simply the publisher of Russian classics; he was now constructing an ideal library that would soon become a library of world literature.

Also in 1931, Jacques Schiffrin opened the *Galerie de la Pléiade*, at the headquarters of the *Éditions de la Pléiade*, where several shows would be organized, mainly photographic exhibitions. Until 1937, when the gallery closed, Schiffrin would act as both publisher and curator, as he had been educated by Bernard Berenson and Henri Piazza.

The *Bibliothèque de la Pléiade* was an immediate success. Ten volumes were published between 1931 and 1932, and Jacques Schiffrin soon needed more capital. As André Schiffrin wrote, his father "quickly used up what little capital he'd managed to put together thanks to investors (mainly from his family and friends), and he did not have the cash flow necessary to pay for his print runs in time."[24] The situation was made even more difficult, as Schiffrin was not spared the economic uncertainty caused by the Great Depression, which also affected the publishing world. As the historian Alban Cerisier describes,

> All levels of publishing experienced a true massacre between 1932 and 1935, especially among the youngest members of the profession. The market seemed saturated with new works and output was disproportionate to demand. . . . Publishing houses disappeared, handing over their stock to more stable companies, which could rely on a diversified production and a well-structured catalog.[25]

Given the need for new financing, it was unlikely Schiffrin would be able to continue his publishing venture on his own. And so he joined forces with a larger publishing house. In 1933, Schiffrin became associated with the publisher Gaston Gallimard.

In 1911, Gallimard, along with the writers André Gide and Jean Schlumberger, founded a book publishing wing of the *Nouvelle Revue Française*. In 1919, shortly after the end of the First World War, Gallimard transformed the *Éditions de la Nouvelle Revue Française* into the *Librairie Gallimard*. Even though the *Nouvelle Revue Française* continued to be published as a literary magazine, from this point on, the books would be Gallimard's responsibility, supported primarily by his brother, Raymond. With André Gide as the leading light, along with two other major figures in French literary life, Jean Paulhan and Jacques Rivière, the publishing house quickly grew. After having missed out on publishing the first volume of Proust's *À la recherche du temps perdu* (*In Search of Lost Time*)—*Du Côté de chez Swann*

(*Swann's Way*) in 1919, Gallimard published the second volume, *À l'ombre des jeunes filles en fleurs* (*In the Shadow of Young Girls in Flower*). The book won the Prix Goncourt, the most prestigious prize in French literature, which would be the first of many for Gallimard. The books Gallimard was publishing embodied a new type of literary French classicism, characterized by the kind of skillful language found in Paul Valéry's works. Soon, many avant-garde authors were also published by Gallimard, such as Antonin Artaud, André Breton, and Henri Michaux. Gallimard was also responsible for the first translations of Freud into French. At the end of his life, Gaston Gallimard could state, with only some exaggeration, "I am French literature."[26]

Not surprisingly, Gaston Gallimard and Jacques Schiffrin moved in the same social circles. Since 1926, within the *Librairie Gallimard*, Boris de Schloezer, Schiffrin's associate at the *Éditions de la Pléiade*, had managed a collection called *Jeunes Russes* (*Young Russians*). Gallimard and Schiffrin also shared an enthusiasm for literary quality and a keen sense of how the era was evolving. But it was André Gide who became an important link between the two men.

A writer published by Gallimard and one of Gallimard's closest friends, Gide was also Schiffrin's friend, with whom he had published Pushkin's *La Dame de pique* (*The Queen of Spades*, 1923), launching the *Éditions de la Pléiade*. In his *Journal*, Gide notes in 1943 that along with Jean Schlumberger, he was the one who originally suggested that Gallimard buy the *Pléiade*: "It was this collection, created and managed so intelligently by Schiffrin, that Jean Schlumberger and I went to so much trouble to get accepted. It was necessary to insist and to fight for nearly two years before reaching an agreement."[27]

And so, in the spring of 1933, Gallimard bought the catalog of the *Bibliothèque de la Pléiade*. On July 31, 1933, a three-year contract was signed, with Schiffrin remaining director of the collection. In the same year, André Malraux's novel *La Condition humaine* (*The Human Condition*) was published by Gallimard and won the Prix Goncourt. Jacques Schiffrin had joined the publishing house that was becoming the most important in French publishing.

For Schiffrin, this was a great accomplishment: In just ten years, he had become one of the most respected publishers in Paris. With the help of Gallimard, the *Pléiade* expanded to reach a wider public, and Schiffrin no longer had concerns about financing the works he published. For Gallimard, the *Éditions de la Pléiade* was a vehicle for showcasing excellence and quality. Gaston Gallimard and Jacques Schiffrin both seemed content with their agreement and in 1936 renewed their contract.

While Jacques Schiffrin's professional career was blossoming in the 1920s, his personal life was also changing in several important ways. In 1922, shortly after settling in Paris, he married Youra Guller, a well-known pianist of Russian origin who had taken first prize in the *Conservatoire de Paris* competition in 1909. The couple became friends with André Gide and other important French literary figures. They separated in 1928, and soon afterward, on June 28, 1929, Schiffrin remarried, this time to Simone Heymann, the woman who would become his lifelong companion. They met when Simone became a secretary at the *Éditions de la Pléiade*. Famed for her great beauty—André Malraux called her the most beautiful woman in Paris—Simone had been born in Neuilly, a wealthy suburb of Paris, in 1906. Her maternal family were among the Jews who had fled Portugal in 1492 and ended up in Holland; her father was a poor street peddler from Alsace. The couple lived on the Left Bank in the chic seventh arrondissement of Paris, at 83 rue de l'Université, in a beautiful apartment behind the Chamber of Deputies, a few blocks away from Gallimard's headquarters on the rue Sébastien-Bottin, where they entertained the most famous literary figures in Paris. On June 14, 1935, their family grew with the birth of their son, André.

Among the many changes in Jacques Schiffrin's life, on January 27, 1927, under the presidency of Gaston Doumergue, Schiffrin became a naturalized French citizen. After more than five years as a resident of France, having married a Frenchwoman, and influencing its national culture, he officially became French. Married, professionally successful, and officially French, Jacques Schiffrin was able to confidently look to the future. Moreover, he was a member of a prestigious network of important people. A few weeks after his naturalization, on March 1, 1927, he received a letter from President Doumergue thanking him for sending him a specially dedicated copy of Paul Valéry's *Essai sur Stendhal*, which Doumergue considered a "true work of art".[28]

The establishment of his longtime friendship with André Gide was also a crucial development at this point in Schiffrin's life. Gide, who was very interested in music, knew Schiffrin's first wife, Youra Guller, quite well. But the tight-knit friendship between the two men went far beyond Jacques and Youra's relationship during this period. The two collaborated on a number of projects, including the translation of Pushkin's *The Queen of Spades*, first published by the *Pléiade* in 1923. In 1928, in his correspondence with the novelist and critic Edmond Jaloux, Gide talks about their budding friendship and his respect for Schiffrin's work:

> I did much more than lend my name to this translation; it took a lot of patience and very detailed work. It was even more difficult as I don't know a single word of Russian, and without Schiffrin's collaboration, it goes without saying that I wouldn't have been able to do a thing.[29]

In his biography of André Gide, Frank Lestringant describes how their friendship began:

> It was at the very beginnings of the Pléiade Editions that he first made contact with Gide, who asked him to help translate Pushkin's *Queen of Spades*. Gide, who didn't know any Russian, was tasked with turning Schiffrin's literal translation into elegant French. The book came out in March 1923 and was the beginning of a fruitful collaboration between writer and publisher: both of them loved beautiful books.[30]

Their friendship, which neither time nor distance would diminish, was strengthened in 1936, when Gide accompanied Schiffrin to the USSR, the only time Schiffrin ever returned to his place of birth. During this trip, Schiffrin was Gide's friend, interpreter, and secretary, allowing Gide to write one of his most important political works: *Return from the USSR*, a criticism of the Soviet regime. Jacques Schiffrin's friendships with French literary personalities such as Gide and Martin du Gard, as well as with Russians in exile like Alexeïeff and Boris de Schloezer, meant he had people he could count on when the horrors of war would force him into exile, bringing Schiffrin's happy years in France to an end.

The war would bring great upheaval to Jacques Schiffrin's life. It forced him on a journey the destination of which was unknown. As a Jew in Nazi-occupied France, he had no choice but to leave. Despite enormous obstacles, Schiffrin would eventually cross the Atlantic to join the "democratic Paris-on-the Hudson,"[31] which was then being created in New York. Schiffrin was thus twice exiled in his life: A Frenchman born in Russia, he would become a Frenchman of Russian origin in the United States. Baku, the Ithaca of this modern Ulysses, was never so far away. Nearly fifty years old at the beginning of the Second World War, Schiffrin would have to again rebuild his life, find work, and learn to speak a new language: English. Schiffrin would do all this and more. Through the strength of his mind and his love of books and ideas, he would succeed in bringing Europe and the United States a little closer together. In a century of darkness, this boy from Baku became a guiding light of modern culture.

1

FROM WAR TO EXILE

W hen the Second World War broke out, Jacques Schiffrin was already a well-known, accomplished figure. He was forty-seven years old, tall, slender, and a familiar sight in the most fashionable Parisian neighborhoods, often accompanied by his wife, Simone. Their four-year-old son, André, was the pride of his parents. Schiffrin was working at the Gallimard publishing house. He had influence with Gaston Gallimard, worked with Gide, corresponded with Paulhan, and was a friend of Martin du Gard. Nevertheless, when hostilities began in Europe, Jacques Schiffrin's life began to fall apart. Initially in the French Army, he lived the life of a soldier, which was harsh but also often boring. It was also in the Army that he showed the first signs of emphysema, a disease that plagued him for the rest of his life.

JACQUES SCHIFFRIN'S "PHONEY WAR"

War was on the horizon. Jacques Schiffrin could sense it, and it caused him a great deal of pain, as was obvious from his reaction when Hitler's Germany took over Austria. The March 1938

Anschluss was on everyone's mind when, in April, Schiffrin went to visit Gide to work on editing the writer's journals, which he kept throughout his life and eventually published. Maria van Rysselberghe, "*la Petite Dame*" ("the Little Lady"), André Gide's lifelong friend and confidant, described this day in her *Notebooks*, which described the day-to-day life of Gide: "April 13, 1938: At the end of the day, Schiffrin came to see Gide. He is terribly upset about what is happening."[1] By October 1938, according to van Rysselberghe, Gide and Schiffrin were discussing what the most appropriate reaction would be in the face of the German threat: "Schiffrin, pessimistic and desperate because he is Jewish, remarks: 'In truth, I've never seen anything like this, Germany imposing its will,' etc., etc."[2]

In spite of the quickening pace of events in the spring of 1938, Gide and Schiffrin continued working together until the end of April: "Schiffrin has come to work with Gide on the index to his *Journal*. He brought several notebooks with the final proofs. Gide was delighted. It was shaping up very nicely."[3]

On September 3, 1939, France and the United Kingdom declared war on Germany after the invasion of Poland. France mobilized troops, and Schiffrin was drafted and issued roll number 1584. Schiffrin served in the Army during what was termed the "Phoney War," which lasted until Germany's invasion of France in May 1940. During this period, there was very limited direct action by the French or British against Germany and only minor skirmishes.

Schiffrin was initially assigned to the Infantry Division in Versailles. On October 1, 1939, he was transferred to the Fourth Regiment of the Civil Defense. In a letter to his friend, the noted Spanish publisher Gustavo Gili, in November 1939, Schiffrin described his daily life:

This life in the barracks, so new to me, as harsh as you might imagine, makes me feel as if I'm dreaming. And just imagine, I'm holding up rather well! Simone and the little one (who is actually a big boy—four years and four months old—and adorable) have been in Paris for a month. I manage to get away from the barracks around six o'clock in the evening and go home until six in the morning. That way, I have the great joy of spending some time with my little family and I even manage to work on some new volumes of the *Pléiade*.[4]

He also described his military experience in his correspondence with André Gide:

I have been a soldier since the first day of the mobilization. A private in the Army, assigned to the Civil Defense. I am with my company in a school. Life in the barracks; our main work is to dig trenches. A rather harsh life that I am coping with rather easily, in spite of the tiredness, the wind, and the Army's great food. Unfortunately, there are few *men* (in the humane sense of the word). Little activity. I came here full of romantic ideas: to serve, to live amongst simple men, etc. I'm disillusioned. I wrote to Giraudoux and saw Duhamel yesterday. If you see them or write to them, remember me to them, if you can. But don't tell them I spoke to you. All I wanted to do was to stay here, behave "like everyone else," but that's becoming far too pointless, and inaction often makes you feel a burden that you can barely stand.[5]

Schiffrin had imagined a "romantic" war, with medieval characteristics, including honor—"to serve"—and the close camaraderie, stripped of the frills of a meaningless life in high society, of "simple men." But the reality was completely different, and Schiffrin became "disillusioned." Gide tried to use his connections to get Schiffrin discharged from the Army. But when Schiffrin discovered what Gide was attempting to do, Schiffrin wrote to him on November 23, 1939, in no uncertain terms: "A note to ask you please not to write anything to D. (Did my letter encourage you to? If so, I expressed myself badly!) I absolutely do not want to leave 'my men' in the barracks to go and work (sic!) with those 'gentlemen.'"[6]

On December 30, 1939, Jacques Schiffrin received a week's leave to get some rest and spend the New Year with his family. He returned to his home in Paris, where he wrote to Gide, "I've just received permission for a week's leave for 'relaxation.' As for 'relaxation,' well, I've been working like a slave. (I'm not complaining: The work keeps me from being depressed!)"[7] Schiffrin continued to work on the new edition of Gide's *Journal* in the *Pléiade* collection with dedication and enthusiasm. But he was nearly fifty years old, and his emphysema was getting worse. After several tests carried out by military doctors, he was finally pronounced "suitable for discharge." On January 12, 1940, he had to appear before one last committee to find out whether he would be demobilized. He received the news the same day: He was officially discharged from the Army after four medical examinations determined that his lungs would never be able to adapt to the conditions of war—not because he had friends in high places. Though he was no longer in the Army, the fate of France and the threat of Nazi Germany weighed heavily on Schiffrin.

Soon after his discharge, Schiffrin met with Roger Martin du Gard at the headquarters of the *Nouvelle Revue Française* (*NRF*). Martin du Gard's description of Schiffrin in a letter to Gide on February 10, 1940, is striking: "I had to stop in at the *NRF* a few times, where I met many people . . . Schiffrin, paler and thinner than ever, looked like a man hunted down by anti-Semitism."[8] And in his *Journal*, Martin du Gard again described him at that time: "Saw Schiffrin, demobilized . . . terrifyingly greenish looking, all skin and bones, very pessimistic, passionately pessimistic.

But still very friendly."[9] Schiffrin was described as an anxious animal, "hunted down," suffering both physically and morally.

From then on, Jacques Schiffrin began imagining a future far from Paris. He wanted to settle in Sartilly, a community in Normandy near the English Channel where he had several friends. From the autumn of 1939, Gallimard had gradually been moving to the property owned by Gaston Gallimard's brother Raymond's wife in Mirande, near Sartilly, following the mobilization for war service of a large number of the publisher's employees. In a letter dated February 6, 1940, Schiffrin wrote to Gide, telling his friend that he had arrived in Sartilly: "Here we are, 'refugees' in a little hotel in Sartilly. . . . Mirande—a charming place that has been invaded by the 'NRF madmen' . . . is three kilometers from our hotel. Gaston is delightful. Here, he seems quite a new person to me."[10] The Schiffrin family arrived in Sartilly on February 3: Jacques, Simone, and André, affectionately called "*Minouche*" ("Sweetie Pie"), who remarked, in his childlike way, of the presence of all the "madmen" of the *NRF*. Their leader, Gaston Gallimard, was also there. Schiffrin's use of the term "refugees" was significant. Though not yet in exile, Schiffrin felt it necessary to leave Paris, a city where he could no longer work, a city abandoned by his colleagues and where he had been overwhelmed by a feeling of pessimism that prevented him from contemplating a possible future. Life in Sartilly, inevitably, was not as exciting as life in Paris. In his correspondence with Dimitri Snégaroff, the *Pléiade*'s printer at the Union Printing Press, Schiffrin described the boredom that overwhelmed his family in Normandy, so far from Paris, while the threat of war hung over them:

Here—no news. I'm resting, thanks to a lack of a telephone, errands and meetings. But this godforsaken place is gloomy, and for my wife, life here is no better than in prison. . . . If this lasts for four or five years, we'll go back to Paris like zombies! . . . But we can't complain. When you think about the people in Poland, Austria, Finland, etc. Ah! My God! When will we finally beat them [the Nazis] down?![11]

From the outskirts of Sartilly, on the coast of Normandy, Schiffrin continued to work on editing André Gide's *Journal* and other projects for the *Pléiade*. From a distance, he was also translating Tolstoy's *War and Peace* with Roger Martin du Gard. It is important to remember what Roger Martin du Gard represented at the time to the French, as well as to the global literary scene. Not only had Martin du Gard won the 1937 Nobel Prize in Literature but as author of *Les Thibault*, a searing book about one man's attempts to break away from the Catholic Church, he was considered one of the great humanist novelists of his day, bringing a historian's attention to detail to his sweeping novels of Europe before the First World War. While Martin du Gard was in the Orne region, in Bellême, he exchanged letters with Jacques Schiffrin that reflected the closeness of their friendship. In a letter to Schiffrin dated March 11, 1940, he wrote,

> My dear friend, here are the first results of two hours of work on Tolstoy . . . But first, let us honestly lay down the most important rule: We must set aside all our mutual sensitivities, once and for all, to be able, without shame, to consider each other "damned fools," with the frankness of old friends who no longer have anything to fear in their differences of language, and this to keep their friendship safe and sound. Agreed? . . . I'd like to know if you're enjoying Sartilly, if your wife is well and if the fresh air is getting rid of the toxins in your body. . . . It could be enormously beneficial to you all to spend a year or more in the countryside![12]

In the same letter, he talked about collaborating on a translation of Chekhov, then about the translation of an unpublished
work by Tolstoy.

In Normandy, Schiffrin worked, socialized with the Gallimards, corresponded with Gide and Martin du Gard, spent
time with his family, and kept abreast of the progress of the war
that threatened to engulf France. As he wrote to his printer,
Snégaroff, "What other infamies will they (the Krauts) come
up with? What monsters! Ah! It will be a happy day when we
have them by their throats! I live only in the hope of seeing that
day!"[13] In April, the Schiffrins left the Hôtel Chesnay in Sartilly
and went to Saint-Jean-le-Thomas, a seaside resort a few kilometers to the west of Sartilly, where they stayed at a hotel called
La Grande-Auberge.[14]

On May 10, 1940, France came under German attack. The
German offensive succeeded quickly, and, within a month,
France was defeated. On June 14, Paris was occupied. On the
seventeenth, Marshal (*Maréchal*) Philippe Pétain, who believed
that further fighting was futile, was appointed prime minister.
He announced that the French "must cease fighting," and on
the twenty-second, an armistice was signed between a humili-
ated France and Nazi Germany. The country was divided in two:
occupied France, to the north of the Demarcation Line, and what
became known as the "Free Zone," to the south. While most
of the "*NRF* madmen" left Mirande in June to go to Carcassonne, in the Free Zone—Jean Paulhan and Gaston Gallimard
joined André Gide there—Schiffrin did not go with them. With
France officially defeated, the Schiffrins remained in Normandy,
hesitant to return to occupied Paris. In his autobiography, André
Schiffrin—then five years old—explains that he and his parents
did, however, return to Paris shortly after the Germans captured

the city to recover certain personal effects before their elegant apartment was requisitioned by the invaders:

> Shortly after the Germans marched into Paris . . . they took over our apartment and we had to leave Paris. To me, our encounters with the German soldiers, even in Normandy, where we first took refuge, were pleasant enough. I remember the friendly young soldiers who, in those early months, were under strict orders to ingratiate themselves with the local population. Being polite, even flirtatious, to my mother did not require much effort. It was all smiles and blandishments at the outset.[15]

After a brief stay in Paris, the Schiffrins went back to Normandy. While northern France and Paris were occupied by the Germans, Marshal Pétain established a collaborationist government in Vichy, a spa town in the Massif Central. Voted full powers by the National Assembly on July 10, 1940, the far-right Pétain replaced the Third Republic with *l'État français* (the French State), which governed the unoccupied south. Jacques, Simone, and André remained in the Occupied Zone, a few kilometers from Mont Saint-Michel, in Saint-Jean-le-Thomas. There Schiffrin received a letter from Gaston Gallimard, dated November 5, telling him that he was no longer employed by the publishing house.

GASTON GALLIMARD'S BETRAYAL

With France now under German control, the fate of the country's Jewish population was very much in doubt. The Vichy government helped the Nazis by registering Jews and excluding them from jobs. In ways subtle and not so subtle, French companies and individuals were forced to or willingly collaborated with the Nazi regime and their policy toward Jews. Publishing was no different, and, once again, Jacques Schiffrin's life, as it had been in Russia, was affected by the fate of history. In what would become a defining moment in his life, Schiffrin was fired by Gallimard.

The news was delivered in a straightforward and unceremonious fashion on *Librairie Gallimard* letterhead that stated that the *Librairie* was a limited company with assets totaling 4,800,000 francs. The letter, signed by Gaston Gallimard, was sent from Paris on November 5, 1940:

Sir,

As I am reorganizing our publishing house under new guidelines, I must end your collaboration in the production of the *Bibliothèque de la Pléiade* collection. It is our intention, of course, to honor the terms of our contract.

Yours sincerely[16]

Thus, in a concise fashion, Gaston Gallimard ended Jacques Schiffrin's career within the Gallimard publishing house.

Dismissing Schiffrin without advance warning was typical of the policy of collaboration that Gallimard adopted after the German invasion. In his biography of Gaston Gallimard, Pierre Assouline describes this period: "In these troubled times, the responsibility of the publisher was measured against the amount of available paper. To have some or not. To obtain any, it was necessary to go through the Germans, their demands and whims. So be it. We collaborated."[17] Assouline further notes that Gallimard "threw out the key members of the publishing house: Robert Aron, and especially Hirsch and Crémieux."

In his biography of André Gide, Frank Lestringant describes Jacques Schiffrin's fate and his relationship with Gaston Gallimard in greater detail:

> This pretense of friendship would not stand up to the test of what was happening. . . . At the beginning of November, Gallimard forced him out with no warning. In the meantime, half of France had been invaded, and a shameful armistice signed with Nazi Germany. Schiffrin would bear the brunt of it, distraught, but in truth, hardly surprised. France was his adopted country; he was a Frenchman at heart, and especially a Parisian. He even had a Parisian accent. But he always knew that in France, he was considered first and foremost, a Jew.[18]

Earlier in his biography, Frank Lestringant speaks of the "Aryanization" of the Gallimard publishing house. This was also the term used by André Schiffrin when he looked back on this tragic episode that was such a determining factor in his family's destiny:

> [With] the German occupation of 1940, when the German "Ambassador," Otto Abetz, issued orders for the takeover of key French institutions, Gallimard was among them. The firm was to be "Aryanized." . . . My father was dismissed in a two-line letter from the owner, Gaston Gallimard. Jacques was one of the two Jews in the firm and their departure led to the increasing role of French fascists in running Gallimard.[19]

Despite its size and importance, the Nazi occupiers made no exception for Gallimard. The French Resistance novelist Vercors (real name Jean Bruller), author of *Le Silence de la mer* (1941), wrote that almost all of the Paris publishers "had to give in to the 'diktats' of the occupiers, since their only choice was either to comply or be killed."[20] Gaston Gallimard actually compromised himself less than some other publishers. Unlike Bernard Grasset, for example, Gallimard never "approved of the racist laws of Nuremberg,"[21] nor did he praise Pétain's triumph when the Nazis took over Europe. But it is important to remember that certain people refused to compromise with the invaders at all. For such individuals, there was a third option: publish underground. In 1942, Vercors, who was then an illustrator, and Pierre de Lescure, a writer, decided to create a clandestine publishing house dedicated to the Resistance: *Les Éditions de Minuit*. Gaston Gallimard behaved as most established publishers did: He accepted the demands of the occupiers without much fuss so he could continue to work, to publish, and sometimes even to oppose Pétain and Nazism. But in doing so, he sacrificed Jacques Schiffrin.

What exactly happened? On June 14, 1940, the Germans marched into Paris. By this point, many of its inhabitants had fled, and the city had virtually lost its identity. All publishing activities stopped in the capital, and the German administration quickly imposed extremely strict policies regarding bookstores. By the end of the summer of 1940, an initial list, known as the "Bernhard List," named those books considered to be in opposition to Nazi ideology, which were thus to be withdrawn from bookstores and destroyed.

On June 21, 1940, an anxious Jacques Schiffrin was already wondering what his future within Gallimard would be, as he explained in a letter to his friend and printer, Snégaroff: "I ask myself with great anxiety how much longer the current director of the *Pléiade* might be kept on at the *NRF*."[22] The atmosphere was beginning to feel poisonous.

On October 4, 1940, the "Otto List" appeared in the *Bibliographie de France*. Named for Otto Abetz, the German ambassador in Paris, it listed additional "forbidden" works to be censored. These included works that criticized Germany or racist ideologies, as well works by Jewish authors and opponents of Nazism, such as Thomas Mann, Stefan Zweig, Sigmund Freud, and Louis Aragon. Unlike the "Bernhard List," this new decree was formulated with the collaboration of the union of French publishers, thus allowing for the possibility of a more or less close pact between literary circles and the Nazi government. Moreover, by the middle of October, a censorship agreement had had been imposed, giving the Germans the right to decide which authors' works could be published and sold.

Gallimard, and his prestigious *NRF*, were in the sights of the Germans. Otto Abetz expressed this idea clearly: "There are three powerful institutions in France: Communism, banking and the *NRF*."[23] According to the Germans, Gallimard was going to have to conform to the Nazi project of a new, Jewish-free Europe under Nazi rule by firing Jewish employees working at his various publications, including the *Pléiade*.

On October 9, 1940, while Jacques Schiffrin was still in Saint-Jean-le-Thomas on the Normandy coast and Gaston Gallimard was in Cannes, the *Propagandastaffel*—the propaganda arm of the Germans—sent their military administration in Paris orders to temporarily close four Parisian publishing houses, one of which was Gallimard's *Nouvelle Revue Française*. Their intention, according to the historian Pascal Fouché, was to "purge the management" and "cleanse their output in the interests of the German Reich."

The use of biological terminology—"purge," "cleanse"—was typical of Nazi ideology. Pascal Fouché, a specialist in the history of twentieth-century French publishing, quotes the entire *Propagandastaffel* order "justifying" the closure of Gallimard, the publisher of the influential *Nouvelle Revue Française*:

The ownership shares of the publishing house are mainly in the hands of Jews. Their influence on political and cultural issues was mainly formed by Jews and continues to be reinforced by Jewish directors employed by the company. The consequence of this has been the wide production of anti-German works that contributed greatly in inciting the French people against Germany. The publishing house has been used, along with others, to publicize a group of authors who are clearly leftwing. They have, along with others, successfully used literature for political ends. There is a hint of these effects in the "Otto" list, which is herewith attached. This list includes the titles of 140 publications by the *Nouvelle Revue Française*, which should have been censored as horrifying, disgusting works and taken out of public circulation. It is most important to note, as well, that this publishing house, due to the size of its business and the extent of its production, had every possible advantage to spread its nationalistic literature among the public.

Right up until the German troops entered France, the Jewish directors, Hirsch and Aron, who today are living in the unoccupied zone, were active heads of the company. But there are still Jews active in the *Éditions de la Nouvelle Revue Française*, namely Pierre Seligmann [sic] and Jacques Schiffrin.

Given that the *Nouvelle Revue Française* is the largest and most important publishing house of modern French literature, it seems doubly necessary to clarify the conditions for ownership and carry out a purge amongst the management and, through that, of the publications themselves.[24]

The Gallimard publishing house frightened the Germans. The occupiers feared the company's prestige, and especially the content of their published books, the "horrifying, disgusting works" More importantly, German propaganda seemed to be targeting the influence of Jewish editors at Gallimard. Jacques Schiffrin was explicitly named, as well as Robert Aron, who had been at the *NRF* since 1922, and Louis-Daniel Hirsch, Gallimard's first commercial manager, who had taken refuge in Auvergne.[25] By the time of the missive from the German propaganda office, none were still employed by Gallimard. Another important Jewish figure in the *NRF*, Benjamin Crémieux, had taken refuge in Provence. He would later become a member of the Resistance; he died in Buchenwald in 1944.[26]

Quite apart from the pressures and regulations applied to the publishing business, all of France was affected by the discriminatory measures imposed against Jewish citizens. In the autumn of 1940, the Germans issued a series of ordinances aimed directly at Jews in the Occupied Zone, where Jacques Schiffrin was living at the time. An ordinance dated October 18, 1940, regarding Aryanization required that all Jews report any company they owned, stop all activity, and turn the company over to a temporary administrator. In addition, a sign reading "Jew" had to be displayed in the window of any business owned by a Jew. In the Unoccupied Zone, Vichy was passing its own measures discriminating against Jews. On October 24, in Montoire, Maréchal Pétain met Hitler and affirmed in a radio address to the French people his determination to collaborate with the victors.

It was under such extraordinary circumstances that Jacques Schiffrin, Jewish by birth but hardly practicing, received Gaston Gallimard's letter dismissing him from the company. As André Schiffrin wrote, "My parents, typical secular Jews, were opposed to all religions, following none of the rites or customs of Judaism."[27] Jacques Schiffrin expected the worst. He was very aware of the tragic turn of historical events, a time when the fact of someone's birth could alone become arbitrary evidence of guilt. On November 3, he again wrote to Dimitri Snégaroff: "I'm living in this state of 'a criminal' waiting for his sentence to be announced. It's terrifying. . . . Will you be obliged to put a 'sign' on your door? (I'm referring to the new laws.)"[28] Two days later, Gaston Gallimard would dismiss him.

Paradoxically, the German military administration in Paris would temporarily close Gallimard, locking its doors on November 9, 1940, four days after Gaston Gallimard sent Jacques Schiffrin his devastating letter. Can we assume that Gaston Gallimard did not act quickly enough for the Germans? Did he not appear obedient enough? According to Pascal Fouché, a note in the transcription of a report dated November 11, 1940, by the official responsible for closing Gallimard explained, "The publishing house was closed in spite of the objections of the management according to whom all Jewish influence had been eliminated and who had for a long time been working with the *Propagandastaffel* in Paris to restructure its business."[29]

In other words, in the negotiations between the directors of Gallimard and the German military administration, the argument that Gaston Gallimard had cut ties with Jacques Schiffrin was used as evidence of Gallimard's obedience to the occupiers. Moreover, a few weeks earlier, at the end of September, Gaston Gallimard had further given in to the Nazis' wishes by agreeing to allow Pierre Drieu la Rochelle,[30] the talented writer but also well-known fascist and friend of Otto Abetz, to take over from Jean Paulhan as head of *La Nouvelle Revue Française*.

So why was the company closed on November 9? To Pascal Fouché, the answer was simple: It was a matter of "pure and simple bravura," a show of power.[31] Even though Gallimard had completely fulfilled the conditions of collaboration required by the Nazi regime's propaganda department, the Germans wanted to assert their power over one of the most important French publishers. The company would not be closed for long, however. On November 28, the *Propagandastaffel* boasted of having come to an agreement with Gaston Gallimard, an agreement that had, in fact, been concluded much earlier. In a letter dated November 28, 1940, from the *Propagandastaffel* to Gaston Gallimard, the Nazi occupiers emphasized the question of "guarantees" and the "interests of collaboration":

> Taking into consideration the past history of your publishing house, and, in particular, because of its very great output, which was especially poisonous and anti-German in tone, the German authorities were obliged to close your publishing house on 11/09 and, following that, to discuss with you the guarantees you could give so that in future, there would be no publication released that was unacceptable to the interest of collaboration between the two peoples and the German Reich, concluded between the *Führer* of Greater Germany and the French Head of State. . . . We inform you, moreover, that your publishing house will immediately be reopened and that for this reason, you may once again resume operation.[32]

To continue to exist, to continue publishing works, to be well looked upon in Paris, Gaston Gallimard agreed to the German conditions imposed in the autumn of 1940. His letter to Jacques Schiffrin on November 5, 1940, is one of the most striking examples of his acceding to Nazi demands. Because Schiffrin was Jewish, Gallimard excluded the man with whom he had spent the first months of the year in Normandy, the man who had worn a French Army uniform during the Phoney War, and the man who had established the *Pléiade*.

The fact that Gaston Gallimard wanted to save his publishing house during the Second World War—a company that was and remains today one of the greatest repositories of French literature—is understandable from a practical point of view.

Given the circumstances, would Gallimard have been able to continue to work in occupied Paris if he had kept Schiffrin on? Probably not. After France was liberated in 1944 and until 1951, a variety of "purges" and prosecutions put thousands of suspected collaborators on trial, including Gallimard. However, Gallimard's case was dismissed since there was insufficient evidence to condemn him, and he was exonerated in 1948.

The fact that Jacques Schiffrin had to leave France and live in exile was less due to Gaston Gallimard than to the German invasion and the policy of collaboration established by Maréchal Pétain. Nevertheless, by accepting Nazi Germany's conditions, Gaston Gallimard abandoned people who had placed their confidence in him and entrusted him with their most precious accomplishments, as Jacques Schiffrin had done with his *Pléiade*. He abandoned his life in France to live in exile and to embark on a journey filled with suffering, the extent of which could certainly not be anticipated at the time. And so, when the few lines of that letter of November 5, 1940, from Gaston Gallimard to Jacques Schiffrin, are re-read, it is understandable to think that Schiffrin had been betrayed. Gallimard boasted of having been party to a "merging of minds," which he appears to have sacrificed on the altar of a more expedient political reality.

Jean Paulhan replaced Schiffrin as director of the *Pléiade*. Schiffrin, gracious even in the face of injustice, recommended him to Dimitri Snégaroff, his printer of choice for the *Pléiade*. In a letter dated December 22, 1940, Schiffrin passed on the torch to his friend: "My dear Snégaroff, As I am no longer working on the *Pléiade*, I asked my friend Jean Paulhan to take over from me. Treat him as you have treated me. . . . I bequeath you my friend Paulhan, who will be a wonderful colleague for you. Welcome him as an old friend."[33]

Paulhan would also treat Snégaroff as if he were an "old friend." In fact, a few days before the notorious roundup of Jews during the *Rafle du Vel d'Hiv*,[34] in July 1942, Paulhan warned Snégaroff of the danger, undoubtedly saving his life.[35] At the end of Schiffrin's letter to Snégaroff in December 1940, he added a postscript that reveals the state of mind of the dismissed publisher: "P.S. I am probably going to leave soon."[36]

LEAVING FRANCE

By the end of the autumn of 1940, Jacques Schiffrin was losing hope. France, his adopted country, was in the hands of Nazi Germany. Gallimard had dismissed him because he was Jewish. So Schiffrin tried to reestablish links with people he felt close to. On November 9, 1940, he wrote to Jean Paulhan, "We are stagnating here in utter solitude. . . . I have a lot of time on my hands—and no idea what to do with it, incapable of shedding a sense of anguish and disgust."[37] The Schiffrins were still in Normandy but soon returned to Paris. In a letter to Jean Paulhan, we learn that the family was living with Jacques's friend Paul Ackerman, a Jewish painter born in Romania, and his wife: "We are staying with a friend: Our rooms are freezing cold and we haven't an ounce of coal. . . . Here is our address: chez Mme Ackerman, 100 Fbg St Honoré."[38] The Schiffrins' apartment on the rue de l'Université had been requisitioned by the Germans, so while the Ackermans agreed to put up Jacques and his family in their apartment, the arrangement could be only temporary, providing them with no feeling of peace or confidence in the future.

The Schiffrins no longer belonged in occupied Paris. Feeling hunted down, and with no professional reason to remain in the capital where they had lived so happily just a few months earlier, Jacques Schiffrin made the decision to leave, initially to the south, which no one now believed was any more "free" than occupied France. André Schiffrin describes the trip in his autobiography:

> I don't remember being worried until we prepared to cross from the German-occupied zone of the north to the erroneously termed Free Zone, theoretically under the control of the collaborationist Vichy government. We had fake papers and I had to memorize a new name. I remember sitting in the dark stall of the bathroom in the border post, where I endlessly repeated it to myself, but in the end it was never asked of me.
>
> Once in the Midi, we stayed in St. Tropez in an apartment that my parents had rented for winter vacations in the tower of Château Suffren. My mother and father continued to try to distract me. On one occasion, this led to the only other moment of real anxiety that I can remember clearly: when they took me to see the new Disney movie, *Dumbo*. American films were apparently still available in Vichy France, but like many Disney films, it emphasized children being separated from their parents, and it left me terrified for days.[39]

These words explain the difficulty of the family's journey to the south of France. They had to have false papers, and the anguish described by André Schiffrin over trying not to forget his new name illustrates the all-pervasive fear of the family, who had to leave Paris in secret.

By the end of 1940, the family was in Saint-Tropez, where Jacques Schiffrin was close to his oldest friends, the old guard: André Gide was only a few kilometers away in Cabris, while Roger Martin du Gard was in Nice.

On January 11, 1941, Martin du Gard wrote to Schiffrin:

Stay calm, my dear friend! It is more important than ever to stay
in control! Do not allow yourself to be weighed down by exhaus-
tion and nervousness! You're here in the Free Zone, with all your
friends around you, and that is already not so bad! Be guided
by the climate: Eat, sleep, relax, and get rid of that cough. . . .
My dear friend, you will never know how often I've thought of
you since June! I was so worried when I learned you were still in
Normandy and hadn't fled with the others to Carcassonne. You
know, *you must not lose faith*. I was very disheartened for a long
time. But there's no longer any reason to be. Every month that
passes brings a little more light on the horizon, and reawakens
hope. All will end well! I firmly believe this and I'm telling you
this as a pessimist."[40]

Unfortunately, Schiffrin's reply has never been found; however, Martin du Gard's reassurances are indicative of Schiffrin's
fear. Jacques Schiffrin was suffering, both morally and physically,
with his emphysema becoming a daily burden. In a letter written a week later, Martin du Gard uses a striking expression to
describe Jacques Schiffrin's life: "Get better, calmly and completely, before continuing your nomadic existence."[41]

At the same time as his correspondence with Roger Martin
du Gard, Schiffrin received a letter from André Gide, which
clarifies the family's situation at the time, as well as certain elements of the recent past. On January 11, 1941, Gide wrote to his
old friend,

The news about you sent to me by Gallimard was already very
old and quite vague. . . . Thinking you were in the occupied zone,
I didn't try to write to you. . . . Well! I've found you again! The

friendly, reassuring atmosphere you will find here will soon, I hope, cure your depression; and the clean air of Saint-Tropez will cure your tracheitis.[42]

Between the beginning of the German invasion of France in May 1940 and the date of this last letter, January 1941, Gide and Schiffrin had had little, if any, contact. It is impossible to know what Gaston Gallimard had told Gide, his most important author, about Schiffrin. However, this letter reinforces the psychological and physical difficulties Schiffrin was confronting. Gide speaks of "depression" and "tracheitis," symptoms of Jacques Schiffrin's profound melancholy as well as his physical pain. In their exchanges, Gide and Martin du Gard discuss their concern for their mutual friend. In a letter dated January 18, 1941, Gide replies to Martin du Gard: "What you tell me about Schiffrin worries me a lot. Is your news more recent than the letter I got from him the day before yesterday, which said his cough was terrible but that he was living with his wife and son in Saint-Tropez (Château Suffren) where I wrote to him immediately?"[43]

Soon Schiffrin would go directly to Cabris to visit Gide, his "most loyal friend." In a letter from Gide to Martin du Gard dated February 7, 1941, he describes Schiffrin as "deeply distraught."[44] Schiffrin's state of despair was also described by Maria van Rysselberghe, who was present when Schiffrin visited Cabris, as she wrote in her *Notebooks*:

February 5: Schiffrin came from Saint-Tropez to see Gide; they're coming to have tea with us; he is unbelievably thin, consumed by worry and visibly in pain; seeing him, I now understand so many things already heard and written, all of which differ only in the details, in the way each person has described it.

Deeply depressed, Jacques Schiffrin finally decided to leave for the United States. At least, that is what he told his closest friends. On February 9, 1941, Roger Martin du Gard sent Schiffrin a letter "about the Antilles." In this letter, which Martin du Gard wrote "might be useful to some,"[45] he gave Schiffrin information about ways to travel to the United States via the Antilles. On February 15, in a letter to Gustavo Gili, Schiffrin discussed recent events without going into detail: "I'm a little tired. I no longer have my work. . . . And as it is very difficult, if not impossible to find work at the moment, I'm making plans to leave for the United States." However, Schiffrin assured his colleague from Barcelona that his departure "is not definite for the moment."[46]

Jacques Schiffrin had been fired from Gallimard only three months earlier, and no one had any idea how long the war might last. The family's day-to-day life was full of uncertainty, and it was in this climate that decisions were made, as this letter from Gide on February 22 makes clear:

I wish that all your anxiety about an eventual departure could be alleviated—and I fervently hope that you won't be called upon to take advantage of the possibility to leave. Yes, I would regret it very, very much if the three of you were to leave. I continue to believe (along with the people in my circle) that your fears are greatly exaggerated. We've heard that Gaston Gallimard will soon be coming back to Cannes. I'm going to push him as far as I can; I want to clearly understand his frame of mind (where you are concerned), his feelings and his plans. I do not at all agree with your dismissal. . . . To me, there is something unacceptable about it, against which both my mind and heart protest.

While waiting for the situation to be "made clear," I want you to be reassured that there are possibilities for you to leave, and hope you will calmly wait, thinking only of regaining your strength, courage, hope and serenity. It is a lot to ask; but I think that your depression is (also) in great part due to your physiological state and that it is your body that must be healed first.[47]

This letter indicates that Jacques Schiffrin had decided to leave, but there a certain naïveté on Gide's part is also evident. The writer, like many French intellectuals, did not seem to fully understand what was at stake at the time, as is evidenced by his belief that Schiffrin's fears were "greatly exaggerated." Gide's optimism was at odds with the reality of the situation in France. In the press, as in the government, anti-Semitism was running rampant. Nazi Germany was setting itself up in Europe as a long-term ruler. Opportunities seemed nonexistent for Jacques Schiffrin, both personally and professionally. With his wife and five-year-old son, could he realistically hope to have a future in the France of 1941? As for Gide, he contributed to the first issue of the *NRF* under the direction of Drieu la Rochelle, published on December 7, 1940. Many people held this against him, but he eventually ended his collaboration with the literary review, which was now under the direction of a writer backed by the Germans. And, in a letter to Schiffrin, Gide's virulent denunciation of Gallimard's decision to dismiss his friend appears to be a genuine demonstration of friendship: "To me, there is something unacceptable about it, against which both my mind and heart protest." But could Gide change anything? He claimed he wanted to push Gallimard as far as possible, yet it is clear that the publisher's decision to fire Schiffrin and other Jews was final and that pragmatism had won out. As long as the Germans held Paris, Schiffrin would have no place at Gallimard. But even more importantly—and this is what Gide did not seem to understand—as long the Germans held Europe, Schiffrin would have no place on the continent.

Schiffrin knew he had to leave to survive. On February 19, 1941, he went to the prefecture in Draguignan, in the Var region of southeastern France, to request a visa for him and his family to go to the United States.[48] Meeting the needs of his family had become too difficult, and earning a decent living in France had become impossible. In New York, he hoped to find work and start a new life, following the example of his brother Simon, a movie producer, who would leave Lisbon for the United States on March 15, 1941. At the time, Schiffrin's sister Hélène (known as Lyolene) had already been living on the other side of the Atlantic for nearly two years, "where she has a good job" as a dressmaker in Kansas City, Missouri.[49] Jacques Schiffrin had to think of himself and the future of his wife and son: "Getting some money and obtaining visas: These were the two requirements for a possible departure."[50]

Thus began a period of great anguish and complications for the Schiffrins, as André Schiffrin has written: "From St. Tropez, my father traveled to and from Marseille, hoping to somehow book passage on a ship to America. But we were to find ourselves trapped for months, anxiously waiting. It was a time of heartbreaking false starts, waiting for exit visas and tickets, each threatening to expire before the others were obtained."[51]

In truth, André's father was bored and had seemed to lose sight of the point of his existence, as he wrote to Gustavo Gili from Saint-Tropez on March 22, 1941: "What can I tell you about us, my very dear friend? We are currently living in a state of waiting for this departure. And we could be waiting a long time. . . . And it is very painful to live like this without any work, for days and months. . . . If we don't manage to leave, I wonder with endless anguish what will become of us. . . . You can imagine the state I find myself in."[52] And Schiffrin would go even further, a month later, in another letter to Gili:

> As I wrote to you before, I find myself in a state of complete inac-
> tion, and that is horribly painful to me as I'm very used to working
> so much. The days are abominably long and we know no one here
> [in St. Tropez] (and there aren't many people here in general in
> this backwater), and there is too much time to think . . . to think
> always about the same thing. It is truly terrible. We hope we will
> be able to leave soon. But it is difficult, long, complicated. Will
> we manage it? God only knows. . . . My head is empty, my heart
> breaking. I am living in endless anguish.[53]

Unable to practice his profession in France and alarmed by a rising tide of public anti-Semitism, Jacques Schiffrin had no choice but to leave, but to do so, he had to fight national borders and a faceless bureaucracy that would determine whether his family lived or died.

On May 11, 1941, he wrote a long letter to André Gide from the Hôtel du Globe, in Marseille. This letter describes the tragic situation of refugees in search of hope in Marseille during the Second World War:

> My very dear friend,

> We are living in a fantasy world: Five days ago, in Saint-Tropez,
> we received a telegram saying we could leave for the United States
> from the Antilles with a ship departing from Marseille on May 15.
> But to do so, we had to go to Marseille at once. So we spent
> the night packing our bags once and for all (the telegram calling
> for us arrived at seven o'clock in the evening!). You can imagine
> what it was like. . . . Ever since we got to Marseille, we have been

subjected to a new form of torture: Things are happening, then they are not, several times in the same day. I mean, once a certain step has succeeded and we have the luck to have everything we need to get onto a ship (visas, tickets, passports, etc.), the next step fails and all is lost! Unbelievable energy and imagination and everything else are necessary to try to save things that seem lost forever or impossible. I drag myself from street to street in the hope of meeting someone who knows someone, etc. Once or twice, luck (?) helped me, friends I hadn't seen for twenty years who knew someone on a committee, in a consulate, a regional government office, etc. And this is where we end up: at nine o'clock this morning, all seemed lost; now it is eleven o'clock and I just had a phone call telling me that another phone call might bring us news of a solution tomorrow morning. And so, right up until the last moment, we don't know if we'll have everything we need to leave (and certain things are missing that I believed I'd get because of firm promises). It's simply abominable. And Minouche wants to play while all this is going on.

Our life is like a terrible dream. If we do manage to leave, it will be in far from brilliant circumstances. Simone and Minouche will be in a cabin in third class and I'll be in a dormitory. And yet, this is what we dream of, and what I hope for fervently, and in such a desperate way (with horrible discouragement ten times a day), hope that I find a real miracle, God knows where or how.

Perhaps you will receive news from me in a few days saying that everything failed and that we are returning to Saint-Tropez. It is very likely that will happen. And then . . . then I won't know what to do anymore. Start all over again? And is that possible? It seems that the ship on the fifteenth is the last one that is going to leave; at least, we don't know if there will be others. So here we are.

I have neither the strength, nor anything in my heart or mind to express what it means to me to have to leave you like this without having seen you again. . . .

Would you please send this letter to Martin du Gard after you read it? I want this letter to be for both of you. I don't have the strength to write twice. . . .

And we send our very best wishes and most melancholy, affectionate thoughts to all our friends. This letter is not what I would have wished. But I am so tired, so battered. Minouche is singing at the top of his lungs while I'm writing. . . .

Good-bye, my friends, may God protect you.

Yours,

J. Schiffrin[54]

Using phrases and words like "fantasy world" and "torture," Jacques Schiffrin described the traumatic experience of a man who had become a plaything for an unpredictable government, whose destiny depended on visas and ships that left without warning from the Mediterranean. In March, André Breton and Claude Lévi-Strauss had left Marseille for New York via Martinique. But Schiffrin continued to wait in an "abominable" situation living out a "horrible dream." Peggy Guggenheim, whom Schiffrin had met in Florence twenty years earlier, happened to meet her old friend in Marseille. She recalled "never having seen anyone so worried and depressed."[55]

However, Jacques Schiffrin's situation was not entirely desperate. Not everyone was allowed to leave France, but with the right supporters, it was possible to do so. During the Second World War, organizations such as the Rockefeller Foundation established special funds with the goal of facilitating the granting of visas for European intellectuals fleeing Europe. However, the Rockefeller Foundation gave preference to academics, so if Schiffrin was going to get a visa to leave for the United States, it would be with the help of his friend, André Gide. In February 1941, Gide wrote to Varian Fry on his friend's behalf. Fry was

a Harvard graduate and a journalist by profession who worked
with the Emergency Rescue Committee during the Second
World War to help persecuted European figures—not necessarily academics—flee Europe and settle in the United States.[56] Fry
had gone to Marseille in August 1940 and had helped people
as diverse as André Breton, Marc Chagall, Victor Serge, and
the German publisher Kurt Wolff. Before being expelled from
France by the Vichy government, Fry's efforts resulted in the
rescue of nearly two thousand people.

To obtain the assistance of Varian Fry, a recommendation was
necessary. In February 1941, Gide wrote to Fry, using all his con-
siderable influence to help his friend:

Dear Monsieur Fry,

One of my closest friends, Jacques Schiffrin, has plans that I am
asking him to submit to you, and I am happy to detail them for you.

Jacques Schiffrin is the creator and director of the beautiful
Pléiade collection, which you surely know, considered the best edition of our French classics, a collection in which my *Journal* has
recently been published. It is with him that I translated Pushkin's short stories; with him as my companion, private secretary
and interpreter that I traveled to the USSR. . . . This should tell
you how much confidence, esteem and affection I have for him.
Recent events have been very harsh to him, and given the situation he is in, I believe you can help him.

I ask you to please offer him the same welcome you would to
me, with great sympathy.[57]

This letter was a determining factor in Schiffrin's destiny. As
a result of Gide's help, Jacques Schiffrin was added to the list
of people to be rescued by the Emergency Rescue Committee.

Schiffrin was assigned number 1196 on the list, between Mathilde Schierbauer and Albert Schildknecht.[58] But a letter from Gide and a name listed in an official document were still not a guarantee of entry into America. As illustrated by Schiffrin's long letter to Gide on May 11, 1941, nothing was simple in wartime Marseille. This is equally apparent in an official Emergency Rescue Committee report dated September 1941, which describes the "important stages of the committee's development" and allows for a better understanding of Jacques Schiffrin's rootless life in Marseille.[59]

Since February 1941, the principle route to America was through Martinique, which had several advantages: "eliminating all the normal formalities normally required to obtain Spanish and Portuguese transit visas; having a visa to leave France in the shortest possible time; finally, costing much less than was charged to travel from Lisbon to New York."[60]

This was the route taken by the passengers on board the *Paul Lemerle*, which left Marseille on March 25, 1941, about twenty of whom were traveling under the protection of the Emergency Rescue Committee, including André Breton, Claude Lévi-Strauss, and Victor Serge. Jacques Schiffrin would not be lucky enough to take the same route. While "the American Emergency Rescue Committee did most of its work during April and May,"[61] those months were also the time of the greatest uncertainty. People had to be ready to leave on just a few days' notice and whether they could get tickets and visas was uncertain:

> Everything had to be done in an extremely short time. For reasons of maritime safety, the shipping companies only released the departure date of the ships four or five days in advance, and it was necessary to successfully carry out some of the required steps in that amount of time. Many of the people we were protecting had

nothing five days before leaving, no American visa, no exit visa, no ticket, no money, and yet managed to leave, in spite of everything, while others, for example, got their American visa an hour before the ship cast off, and their ticket was given to them on the pier. . . . During this time, morning and evening, in the expectation of leaving, both possible and probable passengers came to storm the office to ask advice, or demand the impossible, while those certain to be leaving came to be reassured from time to time, even asking what they should pack in their suitcases. . . . During these two weeks alone, more than one thousand people came to the American Rescue Center's offices.[62]

This document can be considered a counterpart to Jacques Schiffrin's letter to Gide of May 11. What was being determined in Marseille that spring of 1941 was the fate of hundreds of men and women whose survival depended on crossing to the other side of the Atlantic Ocean, a crossing that was not guaranteed. The American Rescue Center sought to put everything in place to facilitate departures, but in this wartime atmosphere, there was nothing simple about making the necessary arrangements with the authorities in Vichy and the German consulate. People were in doubt and suffering, while the overwhelmed staff at the Rescue Center tried to fulfill the organization's historic rescue mission.

At the end of April and the beginning of May, a few ships left for the United States via Martinique. On April 27, ninety people rescued by the Center embarked on the *Winnipeg*. Thanks to an agreement with the shipping company, it was possible to obtain tickets at a very low price. An agreement had also been made with the American consulate, as well as with the government department responsible for crossings to Martinique. At the beginning of May, the same procedures allowed two other ships, the *Mont Viso* and the *Wyoming*, to depart.

On Jacques Schiffrin's passport is a stamp dated May 15, 1941, signed by the "Special Commissioner of the Ports," confirming that Schiffrin was "allowed to embark."[63] The previous day, Schiffrin had received an immigration visa from the American vice-consul in Marseille, Lee D. Randall, which complemented his visa to leave France for the United States granted by the government department in Draguignan on March 31, 1941. Similar stamps were found on the passports of Simone and André Schiffrin. It was done: The Schiffrins were finally leaving. Right up until the day before, they hadn't known whether they would manage to board the *Wyoming*, a name that conjured up the new horizons mentioned in Schiffrin's letter to André Gide dated May 11.

André Schiffrin recounts a disturbing event that took place as they were leaving:

> The departure from France could not have been more humiliating, though everyone was vastly relieved to be on their way at last. Though my mother did not mention it until much later, she was greatly shaken by the shouts of "dirty kikes" that were hurled at us by the longshoremen as our ship left Marseille. Such a betrayal by our countrymen seemed unthinkable and [was] deeply hurtful.[64]

This experience would have been a humiliation, a note of hatred, and a final moment of rage for Jacques Schiffrin, who, in spite of himself, was forced to leave the country he had loved.

The Schiffrin family looked at France one last time, the country that had been synonymous with so much promise and joy, where Simone and Jacques had met and where André had been born. Could Jacques Schiffrin have imagined on May 15, 1941, that he was walking on French soil for the last time? It's impossible to know, and in any case, on board the *Wyoming*, he no longer had the strength to ask himself such questions. After suffering the insults of the dock workers in Marseille, perhaps he recalled the words he wrote a month earlier to his friend, the publisher Gustavo Gili: "The idea of leaving, of starting everything over again, is quite terrifying. But it is, I think, the best, if not the only solution for us."[65]

Soon after the Schiffrins left France, the situation worsened for Jews living there. The first deportation from France to concentration camps took place on March 27, 1942, from Drancy to Auschwitz. In 1940, 333,000 Jews were living in metropolitan France, two hundred thousand of whom were of French nationality. Seventy-six thousand Jews were ultimately deported during the War. Even though mass deportation did not start until 1942, several laws against Jews, as the Schiffrins knew, had been enacted since in 1940. The Jewish status law of October 3, 1940, excluded Jews from the Army, the press, and commercial and industrial jobs.

Everything was happening very quickly: Scarcely a year before, Schiffrin had been director of the *Pléiade*. Since then, the publisher had experienced betrayals, the loyalty of some friends, and the dreams of a future far away, all the while moving from place to place: His apartment in Paris had been requisitioned, so he went to Normandy, then Saint-Tropez, then Marseille. Perhaps, on the *Wyoming*, alongside the pianist Erich Itor Kahn or the sociologist Gottfried Salomon, he began dreaming of reaching Manhattan's skyscrapers, of his son's future, of a land of opportunity that would welcome his family with open arms. Or perhaps, as the *Wyoming* sailed through the Mediterranean toward the Strait of Gibraltar, he was remembering the Baku of his youth, the black gold of the Caspian Sea, or the *Vedenetz* described in the stories he had been told as a child.

Casablanca

While it seemed as if the Schiffrins could finally count themselves lucky, free to go to the United States after long months
of waiting in the south of France, a new problem was about to
stop their journey. The *Wyoming* would never reach the shores of
America. It was suddenly stopped, after only a few days at sea,
and forced to return to Casablanca.

The reasons for this are clear in a Rescue Committee report:

> First there was the incident concerning the *Winnipeg*. The ship
> was stopped off the Antilles and boarded by the English, diverted
> from its course, then taken over. To avoid further such incidents,
> the French authorities forced the *Mont Viso* and the *Wyoming* to
> turn back; they never got farther than Casablanca. The passengers
> disembarked and were interned in camps; the journey seemed to
> have been abandoned.[66]

Beginning in August 1940, shipping between Vichy French
ports and the Antilles had been interrupted by a blockade
imposed by the British in an effort to keep strategic supplies
from reaching the Germans. The British Admiralty was seiz-
ing ships coming from France that were making their way to
the Caribbean to cut the link between metropolitan France and
the Antilles, in the hopes of obtaining Vichy surrender there. In
1942, the United States also began participating in the blockade. This posed a major problem for the Rescue Committee:
How were they to operate when allies, though having a legitimate reason, ruined rescue plans that had been worked out over
several months? From that point on, the French authorities
refused to take the slightest risk and chose to immediately stop
any ships leaving for the United States via Martinique. This is

what happened to the *Wyoming* in June 1941. The ship ended up stranded in Casablanca, the most important city in the French protectorate in Morocco.

André Schiffrin describes this event in his autobiography:

> We were once again stranded, and this time it looked as if there would be no escape, since the Vichy government still controlled Casablanca (as everyone who has seen the film *Casablanca* knows). Claiming a dearth of hotel rooms in the city, the Vichy government forced all emigrants to Morocco to stay in internment camps in the desert. Once again, my father had to scramble for tickets on another ship even as our money ran out, and once again he had to enlist the help of every connection he could. And once again it was Gide who came through, not only with financial assistance but with the offer of a friend's apartment in the city.[67]

In the same passage, he speaks of the "dreadful anxiety" as his father waited, trying to obtain new tickets. In this Moroccan port of call, André Gide would again be involved, as well as Gustavo Gili, the publisher from Barcelona. Jacques Schiffrin was trying to use his personal connections while in Casablanca, which was to become a city of resisters, traffickers, dreamers, and the desperate during the Second World War.

The Schiffrins arrived in Casablanca at the end of May. What was expected to be a short delay lasted so long that it became apparent that the passengers would be going no farther. In a letter to Gustavo Gili, dated June 16, 1941, Schiffrin described these events:

> My very dear friend,
>
> You will be astonished to see a letter from me from Casablanca. We have been put through a terrifying ordeal. After incredible

efforts, we managed to leave Marseille (a month ago) on a cargo
ship leaving for Martinique, from where we were to continue to
New York. Bad luck would have it that our ship was no longer
allowed to leave! So we have been stranded here, for more than
three weeks—in horrible conditions. All this (absolute lack of
sanitary conditions, the slightest comfort, etc.) would be nothing,
if we could only continue on our journey. But for the moment,
we are truly caught between heaven and earth, and we have absolutely no idea what else lies in store for us.[68]

It was not until mid-June, when the stop in Casablanca became
definitive, that Jacques Schiffrin would call on his friends to
come to his assistance.

After disembarking, Schiffrin had to find a way to stay out of
one of the many internment camps to which the various cast-
aways from the *Wyoming* had been sent. Schiffrin needed contacts, people who could offer them a place to stay, but he also
needed money. Initially, Schiffrin sought help from Raymond
Gallimard, Gaston's brother. He wrote to him at the Cavendish
Hotel in Cannes, where the Gallimards were then living, asking him to send 30,000 francs. But Raymond didn't have the
authority to release such a large sum. So it was André Gide,
contacted by Raymond Gallimard, who would take control of
matters, proving his great generosity, as Maria van Rysselberghe
wrote in her *Notebooks*:

June 20, 1941

While I was in Messuguière, Gide telephoned Michaux from
Cannes about something that seemed to upset him a lot. Schiffrin, who was about to reach Martinique, had his ship turned back
to Casablanca, and he sent a telegram to Raymond Gallimard
in Cannes, a distress call, asking him to send 30,000 francs, and

Gallimard has come to Gide. Gide immediately sent a check for 15,000 francs from his personal account through Gallimard, and asked if Loup could send the remaining 15,000 francs at once, advancing him the money until he could arrange for his money to be sent from Paris. And it was done at once.[69]

A week later, it was Gide who told Schiffrin what he had done:

Given the urgency of your request, and not to make you wait any longer—(for I imagined you had your back against the wall—needing this money immediately to perhaps pay for tickets on another ship), so I've asked Mme. Mayrisch for another check for 15,000 francs (by telephone, just now), and she was very willing and happy to help you out. What was essential, as I told Raymond, was to get you the money immediately. We can sort everything out later on. Don't worry about it: I am in no rush and can manage without being repaid in the near future.[70]

While Schiffrin had asked nothing of Gide, turning instead to the Gallimard family who had dismissed him, Gide nonetheless came to the aid of his old friend, even though he did not have vast amounts of money himself, having "all in all only three bank notes to cover my personal expenses and to support Catherine."[71,72] Thanks to André Gide's unfailing support, Jacques Schiffrin received the 30,000 francs essential to survival in a seemingly endless purgatory. While grateful to Gide, Schiffrin became enraged with Raymond Gallimard's seeming lack of honor and charity. Schiffrin wanted to write to Gallimard, but Gide came to Gallimard's defense:

I can assure you that everything Raymond Gallimard told me seemed perfectly plausible and reasonable. If I offered to send the money instead of him it was to save time, thinking that you undoubtedly needed the money urgently—and I have no doubt whatsoever that he will help me get the money back soon. Please don't send him an outraged letter.[73]

Jacques Schiffrin's friends, André Gide and Roger Martin du Gard, who were together when they heard of Schiffrin's problems, quickly sent money and helped him find somewhere to stay in Casablanca. They also sent him the names of their contacts in Morocco. On June 12, 1941, Martin du Gard gave Schiffrin the address of the wife of Raymond Aron, then a young philosopher from the *École normale supérieure*. Suzanne Aron was a good friend of Martin du Gard's and lived in Rabat. Gide put Schiffrin in touch with his friend Jean Denoël, who had founded the literary review *Fontaine* in Algiers in 1939.[74] It was in Denoël's home on the rue Blaise Pascal that the Schiffrins were welcomed in Casablanca. They stayed until they were finally able to leave, later in 1941.[75]

Despite how helpful Gide and Martin du Gard were, it is doubtful that either fully appreciated the danger their friend was in. In his letter of June 12, 1941, Martin du Gard seems to doubt whether Schiffrin's choice to leave France for America was well founded:

I am not underestimating the risks, and I understand your decision, all the reasons that are calling you away toward an active life that had become difficult here. But I have always felt that you were *greatly* exaggerating the risks. The possibility of a useful, working life is not as impossible for you as you might have thought. There could be ways for you to work and live. You have devoted, loyal friends here. I beg of you to calmly be aware of all that; and if rotten luck was determined to ruin all your plans, please have enough lucidity and reason not to be overly disappointed, and stand tall once more against the temptation of excessive discouragement.[76]

Roger Martin du Gard was clearly unaware of the insults hurled at the Schiffrin family by the dockworkers in Marseille, and he had certainly underestimated Schiffrin's humiliation at being dismissed by Gallimard.

Like many French intellectuals of the period, Martin du Gard was blind to the gravity of the threat that Schiffrin and other Jews were facing in France despite the fact that the first wave of arrests of foreign Jews living in France had taken place on May 14, 1941. A second roundup took place on August 20, which also included French Jews.

Nevertheless, Roger Martin du Gard helped the Schiffrins, demonstrating much good will. His letter demonstrates a certain blindness among French intellectuals of the time. In a letter dated July 7, 1941, André Gide seems to express the same feelings:

> Your state of exhaustion is making you see everything as bleak and tragic, things that are unimportant. Ah! If only I could send you some way to calm your mind, I would do so with all my heart! How I wish I could be with you! I am certain that my affection would find the words to bring you peace, hope and even a little reassurance. We would calmly discuss if it would not perhaps be best for you to wait in Casablanca, where you already have some friends; yes, to simply wait, without trying to flee at all costs towards an uncertain future![77]

Yet "uncertain" was already the definition of the present life of the Schiffrin family. And Jacques Schiffrin knew well that the Moroccan protectorate where he was staying took orders from Vichy. Schiffrin's friends were very conscious of the "wrecked existence and gnawing uncertainty" that Martin du Gard described in a letter dated June 26. They all hoped that "if luck would have it that you manage to set sail again, make sure you quickly get your energy back again and feel your spirit being lifted by new experiences."[78]

Operation Barbarossa was launched in late June 1941: Hitler had broken his pact with his allies and sent troops to the USSR. Everyone was now beginning to grasp how much was at stake during this incredible turn of events. For Martin du Gard, it was no longer a question of reassuring his friend; what was happening was far too serious, and it was of a time of great historical importance. In the same letter, he wrote, "We are experiencing the kind of turmoil that humanity has not suffered through in over two thousand years."

In Casablanca, Jacques, Simone, and André found themselves in a situation both strange and anguished. Neither refugees nor in exile, neither at home nor far away, there were living in a kind of purgatory, looking toward the Atlantic, past the Strait of Gibraltar, and yet still under French jurisdiction. But their objective remained the same: to reach New York. But to reach the New World, they had to find a ship and set sail again, hoping they wouldn't be intercepted, wouldn't repeat their misadventures on the *Wyoming*. The correspondence between Jacques Schiffrin and Gustavo Gili is revealing, giving insight into the almost daily steps Schiffrin took to find a solution: a ship that would take his family the United States.

On June 16, 1941, Schiffrin again wrote to Gili saying he had heard of a way out: getting a boat from a Spanish port, Barcelona or Vigo, that would sail to New York.[79] In Casablanca, only one agency was allowed to sell tickets for such a journey: the *Agence Castella*. However, as Schiffrin wrote, he was not the only one in this position: "There are a crowd of people here, who are all in the same situation as us, and who are thronging into the only agency who deals with these mythical departures." So he once again called on his old friend for help:

> I think that the only way to leave here through Spain is if some-one in your country reserves places on a Spanish ship leaving for New York. (The passage could be paid for in New York. My sister and brother are there, and they would cover the cost.) What could you do, my dear friend, to help save us from our great distress?

Traveling in second or third class would be fine for Jacques Schiffrin, who even gives an approximate price range for each ticket: $300 to $350. In Schiffrin's mind, leaving was a matter of life and death.

A few days before, André Schiffrin had celebrated his sixth birthday. "In such conditions!" his father exclaimed. Meanwhile, on June 18, Gustavo Gili, who had not yet received Schiffrin's let-ter of the sixteenth but who had just learned of Schiffrin's situa-tion through a common friend, began making enquiries to obtain as much information as possible. He found out that second-class tickets from Spain to the United States cost $366 per person. Gili even met with the head of a maritime company that offered such an itinerary, the *Compania Transatlantica*. There were very few ships, demand was extremely high, and it looked as if the Schiffrins might have to wait two or three months before they could leave for New York. Ships left from Vigo, Bilbao, and sometimes from Lisbon, and Gustavo Gili offered to put up the Schiffrins in Bar-celona while they waited. On June 23, Gili received Schiffrin's letter of the sixteenth. He replied, trying to reassure his friend: "You can see that your friends are concerned about what happens to you. . . . You have two treasures [Simone and André] who are worth more than all the money in the world; how can you feel miserable? If by chance you are in distress, better times lie ahead for you; be sure of that." Gili also told Schiffrin that one of their mutual friends was en route to New York, where she intended to make contact with Jacques's brother Simon, so he could pay for the Schiffrins' tickets in advance while the family waited in Casablanca. And it was, in fact, Simon who took on the responsibility of paying the family's fares through an agency on Battery Place in New York.

While Gustavo Gili was making an effort to gather reliable information, in Casablanca, Jacques Schiffrin was hearing a different version of events. Whereas Gili considered the *Compania Transatlantica* the only company able to make the crossing possible for the Schiffrin family, Schiffrin was certain the only agency that could organize the journey was the *Agence Castella* in Casablanca. Schiffrin witnessed some of the *Wyoming* passengers leaving Casablanca on voyages arranged by the agency. But at what price! People were prepared to pay $1,200 each to go to New York City. However, Jacques did not despair and confirmed receiving a telegram from his brother Simon saying there was a possibility the family could have places on a ship leaving July 10 from Cádiz in southwest Spain. But it would still be necessary to go through the *Agence Castella*, as no one could leave Casablanca without its permission. Exhausted, Schiffrin wrote to Gili on June 24, "You cannot imagine, my dear friend, how exasperating, harrowing and anguishing all this is. We spend all our time rushing around the city trying to find people who can give us information, help us, etc. And we don't know what to do with the information or where to find any."

Time was running out. The Schiffrins' visas for the United States obtained in Marseille were valid only until September 14. The matter was becoming urgent. If their visas expired, they would be forced to go back to France, the country that had rejected them and where they were in danger of being deported. As Jacques

Schiffrin wrote, "You cannot begin to imagine what kind of life we are living. I can understand how some people go mad!"

Then suddenly, hope. Two days later, on June 26, Schiffrin learned that his brother had reserved and paid for places for the three of them on a ship leaving Cádiz on July 10. There remained, however, one final bureaucratic hurdle: The Schiffrins had to obtain transit visas so they could get to Cádiz a few days before the voyage to ensure they got onto the ship. Schiffrin asked Gustavo Gili if he had any contacts in Madrid who could speed up the process of obtaining the visas.

But fate did not look kindly on the Schiffrins. In a letter to Gili dated July 6, 1941, Schiffrin explained that, once more, their hopes had been dashed: "In fact, despite having places reserved and paid for, we have not received any confirmation. This is unbelievable and incomprehensible, but this is the way it is. Bad luck? Fate? Only God knows." Other people stranded in Casablanca were leaving the next day, or the day after that, but the Schiffrins remained cornered, condemned to remain in a city they dreamed of leaving. More than ever, Schiffrin seemed exhausted and perplexed: "I am really at a loss and don't know what action to take or what to do." For six months, this man, who was nearly fifty years old, had been battling, from Saint-Tropez to Marseille to Casablanca, to save his family's lives by trying to get to New York.

Then there was the possibility of getting on another ship on July 20, which was supposed to leave Barcelona, where Gustavo Gili lived. Schiffrin could hope once more: "Who knows? Perhaps Fate will have us leave via Barcelona and we will be able to see you?!" But fate did not allow Gustavo Gili and Jacques Schiffrin, two publishers caught up in the Second World War, to meet in Catalonia that summer of 1941. Schiffrin would never set foot on the ship destined to leave from Barcelona on July 20.

Given the succession of bad news and terrible luck, Jacques Schif-frin's friends who had remained in France began to imagine the worst. As Roger Martin du Gard wrote in a letter dated July 4, 1941,

> Whatever happens—and I'm thinking of the worst, coming back with nothing—it will be a great relief for you to know you have done both the possible and the impossible. . . . and that you have nothing whatsoever to reproach yourself for in future! And also the feeling that you are capable of "superhuman" effort, for life in France, as dif-ficult as you may imagine it, would never require as much strength of character and willpower as you are showing at the moment![80]

Could Jacques Schiffrin really give up hope? He was in Casa-blanca with his wife and six-year-old son whom he loved, so could he truly think of giving up? There was only one deadline: Septem-ber 14, 1941, the date their visas would expire. The family had to reach New York by that date. Until then, he was prepared to fight with all the strength he had left. He no longer thought about his burning lungs or delicate state of health. From that point on, he used all his willpower for one objective: to cross the Atlantic.

Things soon began to move quickly, however. Correspon-dence between Schiffrin and Gili was reduced to a few tele-grams. On July 11, Schiffrin asked Gili for information about a ship that might make the crossing he desired: the *Ciudad de Sevilla*. On the seventeenth, Gili replied with a short telegram: "*Ciudad Sevilla* probably leaving beginning August. Arrange-ments for passage must be made in Lisbon. Impossible to get anything from Barcelona." On July 25, Schiffrin sent Gili a tele-gram giving him the much anticipated news, so anticipated that he didn't dare believe it himself: "Have got passage on *Ciudad Sevilla*. Leaving Sunday for Tangiers where we should embark 30 July. My warmest wishes, Schiffrin."

The Schiffrins had finally found a ship that would take them to the other side of the Atlantic, where they could begin their new life. Jacques's and Simone's passports are stamped with the seal of this wonderful news. On July 26, they finally left Casablanca, traveling by train along the Atlantic coast to reach Tangiers, where they boarded the *Ciudad de Sevilla*.[81] Departing the port of Tangiers on August 4, 1941, the Schiffrins were free again.

Before stopping at Tangiers, the *Ciudad de Sevilla* had set sail from Barcelona. A friend of Gustavo Gili's son, Elisabeth Katzenellenbogen, had left on the same ship. Gili gave her a letter to pass on to Schiffrin: "I wish you *bon voyage* and good health; stay strong!" Gili also personally knew the captain of the *Ciudad de Sevilla*, Francisco Serra, to whom he had recommended the Schiffrins. Schiffrin met Katzenellenbogen on board, and together they sent their best wishes to Gustavo Gili. After many long months of despair, doubt and bureaucratic battles, Jacques, Simone, and André Schiffrin were finally on their way: on the Atlantic Ocean, headed for New York, the city that was waiting to welcome them.

Crossing the Atlantic

For a long time, the *Ciudad de Sevilla* continually made the journey from Barcelona to Cádiz to the Canary Islands and back. It was nearly 125 meters long and about sixteen meters wide. At full steam, the *Ciudad de Sevilla* could travel at sixteen knots (nearly thirty kilometers) per hour. There were three classes: one hundred thirty-five passengers in first class, fifty-eight in second class, and fifty in third class.[82]

In May 1941, amidst the turmoil of this great moment in history, the *Ciudad de Sevilla* embarked to cross the Atlantic for the first time. It left Barcelona on May 6 and arrived in New York via Lisbon and Havana, transporting some four hundred passengers—nearly twice its capacity—most of them Europeans leaving their continent because of the war. The Schiffrin family was on the *Ciudad de Sevilla*'s second transatlantic crossing, which left Barcelona for New York on August 1, stopping in Tangiers, then Lisbon and Tenerife. This time, 555 people were crammed on board.

In his autobiography, André Schiffrin recalls their critical crossing:

> As far as I was concerned, my only setback during the endless crossing to America was dropping my Donald Duck doll into a puddle of vomit; it became irremediably nauseating and had to be cast overboard. Meanwhile, I was unaware of the horrendous conditions into which my father and the other men were crammed. The ship's owners, having charged vast amounts for a ticket, had crowded as many people as they could into a stifling, airless hold where they were stacked on bunks frighteningly reminiscent of those photographs that later came out of the concentration camps. There were constant fights in this squalid atmosphere as people sought space in which to breathe and live from day to day. In reading Victor Brombert's memoirs, *Trains of Thought*, I saw how commonplace the experience had been. His description of the crossing could have been mine (though he notes that the most aggressive and difficult passengers were those who had been interned in German concentration camps and were determined to protect themselves from their fellow passengers). Basically, each crossing had the same story. The refugees were deprived even of the originality of their suffering. Everyone had the same experience and, as a result, no one spoke about it once in America. After all, we were lucky to have escaped.[83]

As a child, André Schiffrin could not understand the horror of the crossing his father experienced. While André seems to have had a "bearable" journey—probably in a cabin with his mother—his father and the other men on board were crammed together in the hold, in conditions worse than deplorable.

In his *Journal*, Julien Green, who met Jacques Schiffrin in New York, comments on the publisher's crossing: "Part of the journey was spent in the hold."[84] But in a letter sent to Gustavo Gili shortly after his arrival in New York, Schiffrin asked his friend to thank the doctor and the captain of the *Ciudad de Sevilla* who "were charming to us and made our crossing easier."[85] Nevertheless, the experience of the crossing was traumatic. These men and women, rejected by their societies and forced to leave, found themselves treated like animals during a hellish journey before recovering their freedom. Once in New York, some of the passengers stated that they would have preferred to stay in Germany, at the heart of the Third Reich, rather than live through such a crossing.

In his autobiography, André Schiffrin mentions Victor Brombert's memoirs, *Trains of Thought*. A professor of literature at Princeton, Brombert was a native of Russia forced to leave France for the United States during the war. The description he gives of his own Atlantic crossing on board the *Navemar* can help us imagine what Schiffrin's journey must have been like:

> Our *Navemar*, with its heavy hull and depressing appearance was not a passenger ship at all, but a cargo ship that usually transported bananas. This banana boat had cabins for a maximum of fifteen people and there were 1,200 of us crushed into the hold. We were the bananas. That was how we realized how much he had cheated us. . . . We found ourselves prisoners for weeks at a time in this unhygienic cargo ship overcrowded with refugees. . . . The area where our miserable bunks and sinks were found my father called "*ad*," the Russian word for Hell. . . . We were told that the newspapers described the *Navemar* and the nightmarish crossing of human cattle as a "floating concentration camp."[86]

A hell in which sickness was ever present, a reification of individuals who had become "bananas," in sum, "a floating concentration camp": That was the image Brombert retained of his nightmarish crossing. It is virtually the same feeling of being a prisoner, of dehumanization, of a lack of space when men are crushed together that Claude Lévi-Strauss describes in his famous book *Tristes Tropiques*, in which the anthropologist narrates his own crossing:

> I finally got my ticket on the *Capitaine-Paul-Lemerle*, but I only began to really understand it all on the day I was leaving, passing the rows of anti-riot police wearing helmets and holding machine guns who surrounded the dock and prevented the passengers from having any contact with the family or friends who had come with them, cutting short their good-byes with their prodding and insults: This was truly a lonely adventure, more like the departure of galley slaves. Even more than how we were treated, it was the sheer number of us that was staggering. For they crammed around three hundred and fifty people onto a small steamboat that—I went to check right away—had only two cabins and a total of seven bunks.[87]

These were Schiffrin's final weeks of suffering before attaining a goal that was now within reach, but they were also endless days, crammed in, alone, with all humanity stripped away. As André Schiffrin emphasized, the trauma was made twice as bad by the silence. Once they had arrived, the refugees from across the Atlantic didn't dare speak of their experiences—undoubtedly because they considered themselves so fortunate, after so many ups and downs, to finally be on the right side of the ocean. No one talked about it for fear of being considered troublesome, or being perceived as embellishing, or not being listened to.

After two weeks, the family's journey ended. It was August 20, 1941, when Jacques, Simone, and André Schiffrin stepped onto American soil for the first time. They spent the morning on the ship, off the coast of Staten Island, waiting for the quarantine service to check the health of the passengers.

New York was inevitably a surprise, a never-ending adventure. The family's first sight of the city was a far cry from their memories of Baku, Saint-Jean-le-Thomas, Saint-Tropez, Marseille, Casablanca, or even Tangiers. The Schiffrins had never seen anything like it; they were headed for a new life far from the war and horrors of Europe. The *New York World Telegram* of August 21 contains a photograph of André and Simone Schiffrin upon their arrival in New York. Little Minouche was six years old at the time and extremely thin; he looks anxious in his short trousers and little cap. His mother, who had just turned thirty-five, has her arm around his waist. She still has all her Parisian charm and elegance, in spite of the long crossing. She is wearing a suit, her hair is done, and her nails are polished. Jacques Schiffrin is not in the photo. He had spent the crossing in the hold of the *Ciudad de Sevilla*, waiting and in pain; perhaps he was simply too exhausted to put on a show for the photographer.

From this point on, Jacques Schiffrin and his family became refugees in the United States. To get there had taken all his strength and had left him exhausted. However, he could finally breathe again, consoled in the knowledge that he had brought his family to a safe haven. Nevertheless, as he disembarked in a strange country, the giddiness at having his dream come true was no doubt mixed with a sense of what was irreversible: On the other side of the ocean, he had left other family members and friends, and the *Pléiade* had been taken away from him. He had become a man somewhere between a refugee and an exile, and the distinction would always remain extremely fine. But on that August day in 1941, Jacques Schiffrin knew he had a new life to build in America.

Mrs. Simone Schiffrin and her son, Andre, 6, arived from Paris, where Mr. Schiffrin was publisher. They have been trying to book pasage to America since last December.

FIGURE 1.1 André and Simone Schiffrin arriving in New York. (Schiffrin family personal archives).

2

A PUBLISHER IN NEW YORK

On August 20, 1941, Jacques Schiffrin and his family arrived in New York. On that same day in Paris, a roundup of Jews led to the arrest of 4,232 men who were subsequently interned in a makeshift holding camp in a half-finished apartment building in the Paris suburb of Drancy. In the United States, the Schiffrins were safe, far from the war and the anti-Semitism that was devouring Europe, but they still needed to rebuild their lives. Even though Jacques had a brother and sister in the United States, he had left behind an entire world in Paris, a world he had built over nearly twenty years. He had to learn how to cope in this new country, with a new language and a new culture.

When they first arrived, the Schiffrins' English was far from perfect. But, more significantly, it was their relationship to this new world and the strangeness of America that would prove problematic. Of course, the Schiffrins had been able to watch Disney movies and buy their son a Donald Duck toy in Europe, but coming to grips with New York was a very different matter. First and foremost, they had to find somewhere to live and learn how to handle day-to-day concerns. Jacques Schiffrin would soon find work in a field he knew intimately and was passionate about: publishing. Although he would found a publishing house that bore his name, he would later join another man in exile in a more fruitful venture.

In New York, Jacques Schiffrin met Kurt Wolff, a German publisher who invited him to join an enterprise he had just launched in the United States: Pantheon Books. Slowly but surely, the association between Schiffrin and Wolff turned this new publishing house into one of the leading lights in the United States. But most importantly, Pantheon became a bridge between America and Europe, including France. Jacques Schiffrin would also come into contact with publishers in South America and Canada. He was at the center of a publishing network that had become globalized in the years during and immediately following the Second World War. As a publisher in New York, Schiffrin soon became a busy man, in demand to act as an American go-between for several journals. He also corresponded with numerous writers, old friends who had remained in France but who had kept in touch. At the same time, Schiffrin was making his way into New York social circles, especially ones that included other Europeans in exile. However, first, he had many hurdles to overcome.

THE PAIN OF EXILE

Jacques Schiffrin's journey from Paris to New York is similar to those of many French intellectuals, like Breton, Lévi-Strauss, and Maritain, who crossed the Atlantic during the Second World War.[1] But it was also the journey of a man who had already been in exile from his native Baku, a Jew for whom exile was literally a matter of life and death, and a man who was nearly fifty years old when World War II broke out. The question of returning to

France after the war, which was so important to the community of French exiles, became even more significant to Jacques Schiffrin: Unlike the majority of exiles in New York who returned to Europe after the war, he would never set sail for home again.

From his arrival in New York in August 1941 until his death in December 1950, Jacques Schiffrin never felt completely at home in Manhattan. In New York, Schiffrin expressed the sadness of exile, the nostalgia for a lost world. And even though he did not make it known, he lived with that anguish on a daily basis, as his correspondence shows.

Jacques Schiffrin's life mirrors that of the Austrian writer Stefan Zweig, who described his experiences of early-twentieth-century Vienna's rich and dynamic intellectual society and subsequent exile in his famous memoir *The World of Yesterday*,[2] which he began writing in 1934, at the beginning of the Nazis' rise to power. However, while Stefan Zweig never returned from his exile in Brazil (he committed suicide there in 1942), Jacques Schiffrin continued to suffer during his exile, over the random nature of events that had forced him to start life over, yet again.

The events of the twentieth century have given birth to an entire field of analysis on the theme of exile, and many of its most important contributors have been eminent intellectuals who personally experienced the effects of exile. Hannah Arendt had crossed the Atlantic to flee Nazism with the help of Varian Fry's network. A philosopher who wrote about politics and totalitarianism, she also reflected on the question of exile. In her essay "We, the Refugees," she analyzed and clarified the nature of her exile experience while conceptualizing the new status of "refugee" for people who had no choice but to leave Europe:

> In the first place, we don't like to be called "refugees." We ourselves call each other "newcomers" or "immigrants." Our newspapers are

papers for "Americans of German language"; and, as far as I know, there is not and never was any club founded by Hitler-persecuted people whose name indicated that its members were refugees.

A refugee used to be a person driven to seek refuge because of some act committed or some political opinion held. Well, it is true we have had to seek refuge; but we committed no acts and most of us never dreamt of having any radical opinion. With us the meaning of the term "refugee" has changed.[3]

Arendt describes these refugees in a new way, as damaged people who seek nevertheless to behave as if nothing has happened, to become integrated as quickly and in the best way possible, and to establish themselves:

Even among ourselves we don't speak about this past. Instead, we have found our own way of mastering an uncertain future. Since everybody plans and wishes and hopes, so do we.[4]

And yet, a time always comes when the mask is removed, when the hidden past intrudes upon the present:

I don't know which memories and which thoughts nightly dwell in our dreams. I dare not ask for information, since I, too, had rather be an optimist. But sometimes I imagine that at least nightly we think of our dead or we remember the poems we once loved.[5]

Edward Said also described the profound nature of his experience in exile in his *Reflections on Exile*, making a distinction between the concepts of a "refugee" and someone in "exile":

Exile is strangely compelling to think about but terrible to experience. It is the unhealable rift forced between a human being and a native place, between the self and its true home: Its essential sadness can never be surmounted. . . . The achievements of exile are permanently undermined by the loss of something left behind forever. . . .

Although it is true that anyone prevented from returning home is an exile, some distinctions can be made among exiles, refugees, expatriates, and émigrés. *Exile* originated in the age-old practice of banishment. Once banished, the exile lives an anomalous and miserable life, with the stigma of being an outsider. Refugees, on the other hand, are a creation of the twentieth-century state. The word *refugee* has become a political one, suggesting large herds of innocent and bewildered people requiring urgent international assistance, whereas *exile* carries with it, I think, a touch of solitude and spirituality.[6]

And so, Jacques Schiffrin was a refugee, one among the "large herds of innocent and bewildered people" condemned to cross oceans to flee persecution. It is for such people that in 1951—a year after Jacques Schiffrin's death—the United Nations established the Geneva Convention conferring a specific status on refugees and guaranteeing them the rights available in the country that accepts them.

As Edward Said writes,

Much of the exile's life is taken up with compensating for disorienting loss by creating a new world to rule. It is not surprising that so many exiles seem to be novelists, chess players, political activists, and intellectuals. . . .

Like medieval itinerant scholars or learned Greek slaves in the Roman Empire, exiles—the exceptional ones among them—do leaven their environments. And naturally "we" concentrate on that enlightening aspect of "their" presence among us, not on their misery or their demands.[7]

An example of such achievements is Jacques Schiffrin's contribution to the founding of one of the most prestigious publishing houses in New York: Pantheon Books. But if Schiffrin is unique in his contribution to spreading knowledge of European scholarly culture in the United States, he nevertheless remained affected by the melancholy that is part of Edward Said's definition of a person in exile. Said quotes Wallace Stevens, who explains that those in exile have "a mind of winter in which the pathos of summer and autumn as much as the potential of spring are nearby but unobtainable."[8] This describes Jacques Schiffrin's mood in New York, his nostalgia for both the past and future and his mournful sense of disorientation and loss. Such feelings were cruel and ever present in his daily life, forming a reality to which he owed everything, but yearning, nevertheless, for a life that remained painfully absent.

LIFE IN NEW YORK

When they arrived in New York, the Schiffrins checked into a hotel on the Upper East Side, near Jacques's sister Lyolene. The Adams Hotel was located on the corner of East 86th Street, close to Central Park. Though since converted into a residential building, it has retained the original architecture with its twenty-three floors and pyramid-shaped roof. It resembled nothing the Schiffrins had ever seen before.

Living on the third floor of the hotel, the Schiffrins asked their son André to say "Three, please" to the receptionist so the elevator would be sent to the right floor. So he could remember the two words that sounded so foreign and be understood in this new land, Minouche decided to repeat as quickly as possible the similar-sounding French words *"cerise prise"* ("cherry" and "plug").

Their hotel and Jacques's sister being close by were the foundations of the family's establishment in the symbolic capital of the New World. By the time the Schiffrins arrived, New York was also emerging as a global city, serving as a nexus for ideas and people from around the world. The French historian Emmanuelle Loyer writes:

> At the beginning of the 1940s, New York was already an international city rich in culture due to 150 years of intensive, diversified and continual emigration that began in the later part of the nineteenth century and continued into the beginning of the twentieth. The emigration from the war colored even further the human landscape of a city that had gone from 3.5 million to 7.5 million inhabitants between 1900 and 1940.[9]

In New York, Jacques Schiffrin was hardly the only French immigrant. He quickly made contact with other intellectuals who had sought refuge or simply chosen to remove themselves from the violence spreading throughout Europe. Less than two weeks after his arrival, on September 1, 1941, Jacques Schiffrin received a letter from the Catholic theologian Jacques Maritain, who was also in New York:

> Dear Sir,
>
> What joy to learn you have arrived! We knew that you had been held up in Casablanca, and we were very worried about you. Thank you for having written to me. We would be so happy to see you and Madame Schiffrin. As soon as we are back in New York, I'll let you know.[10]

In his *Journal*, the novelist and essayist Julien Green also writes of meeting Jacques Schiffrin in New York:

September 4, 1941

Saw Schiffrin yesterday; he arrived here after traveling for one hundred days, with his wife and little boy. . . . I thought I could make out traces of deep anguish on his face, but also a kind of serenity in his voice and eyes that I had never seen in him before. His dignity and good manners moved me. Here is a person who has been ennobled by hardship. We talked for an hour in a quiet corner of my hotel. He told me that certain areas of Paris would be hard to recognize, like the rue Royale, where a sign forbids French cars from entering. And enemy soldiers everywhere. He sadly confirmed that some of the middle classes agreed to collaborate with Germany and cited the case of a young boy he had known in the past who told him, "I'd collaborate with the devil if I had to."[11]

Julien Green seemed to capture Schiffrin's mood on September 3, two weeks after he arrived in America. Green could see traces of the suffering that those terrible days left: from May 15, 1941, when he embarked from Marseille on the *Wyoming*, to August 20, 1941, the day he arrived in New York aboard the *Ciudad de Sevilla*. But Jacques Schiffrin had lived through more than those days of travel and flight; it had been a long, nightmarish year since the German victory. Nevertheless, there was a counterbalance to the "deep anguish." Green describes in the "serenity" and "dignity" of a man who had fulfilled his obligation to take his family far from the war. Jacques Schiffrin also served as a witness and conduit, bringing news to those already in exile about life in Nazi-occupied France.

On December 6, Julien Green and Jacques Schiffrin met for lunch. Once again, Schiffrin described having seen "German flags everywhere in Paris,"[12] a sight Julien Green hoped he would never have to see.

Apart from the French community of immigrants, Schiffrin also spent time with several Russian exiles in New York, including the engraver Alexandre Alexeïeff. His daughter, Svetlana, remembered meeting Jacques in New York at his brother Simon's house, where they had a wonderful time and spoke Russian.[13] The guests talked about the possibilities of life in New York and discussed old friends, like Gustavo Gili, whom they had both known well since the *Don Quixote* project. Svetlana, then eighteen years old, also recalled having to look after André, whose little cap made him look like a soldier.[14]

Schiffrin also kept in touch with old friends who had stayed behind in Europe; he continued to correspond with them, and they were delighted at the successful outcome of his long journey. On August 31, André Gide wrote to Schiffrin, congratulating his friend on having arrived safely: "What a relief it is to know you are finally beyond the barbed wires of Europe."[15] From Paris in November 1941, Gide and Martin du Gard both wrote to Schiffrin to say they finally understood the danger he had faced.

"All in all, I think you were right to leave," Gide wrote to Schiffrin.[16] In a letter dated November 5, 1941, Roger Martin du Gard wrote virtually the same thing: "The future is bleak. It is some consolation to know that a friend has managed to get away, and that he was lucky enough to escape the disaster that is threatening us all." Jacques Schiffrin was no longer a man with exaggerated fears who took pointless risks and used all his energy in vain. Martin du Gard also described the new world Schiffrin would now be a part of, a world that was as desirable as it was distant: "How far away you are, Schiffrin! Not just on the other side of the ocean, but on another planet, in a land where men are free, where life is still the life we always knew."[17]

Schiffrin also continued to correspond with Gustavo Gili, who had helped him so much when he had been stranded in Casablanca. In a letter dated October 8, Schiffrin talks about his first few weeks in New York and the people he had met: "mainly Frenchmen, either old friends or new people." And in one sentence, he describes his first impressions of his new city: "New York is an enormous city, extremely tiring and very expensive." But, most importantly, Schiffrin expressed his relief: "It is so extraordinary that we managed to get here; we're so relieved not to be over there anymore." But Schiffrin could not forget those who had to remain in Europe during that time of upheaval: "Alas! The news we are receiving from friends and relatives is hardly encouraging, and we think about them constantly."[18] What he had left behind always remained present to him in the news and advice given to him from across the ocean. In a letter dated December 31, 1941, Gili praised his friend's success: "You finally made it to New York, and I hope that God will protect you and that you will quickly be able to create a new situation for yourself that is as prosperous as you deserve, which, given your intelligence and courage, seems very possible."[19]

During their first few months in New York, the Schiffrins also had to resolve their legal status in America, a bureaucratic process that lasted several years. On November 12, 1941, the Schiffrins went to the French consulate in New York, where they received a certificate, renewable every three years, confirming they were legal residents of the United States. A month later, on December 11, the family appeared before the Immigration Department in New York. According to their records, Jacques Schiffrin, publisher, born in Baku on March 28, 1892, was five feet, eleven inches tall and weighed 120 pounds. In 1942, the

American government sent a Registration Certificate card to Jacques Schiffrin, which he had to carry with him at all times. In February 1944, Schiffrin received a Resident Alien's Identification Card from the Immigration Service's Legal Department (what would become known as the "Green Card" in 1946.) While not considered an American citizens, Schiffrin was allowed to become a resident of the United States and was able to work under the same conditions as American nationals. Yet Jacques and Simone remained French: They renewed their Identity Cards at the French consulate in New York in May 1949. No archival material indicates that Jacques Schiffrin ever took American citizenship.[20]

The Schiffrin family gradually settled into a routine of daily life, feeling their way forward. But their days were still filled with worry and doubt. Initially, they had to find somewhere to live, as the Adams Hotel was only a temporary solution. In the end, they found furnished accommodation facing the Hudson River. Jacques was pleased to be able to see the trees and sky from his windows at 62 Riverside Drive, near 78th Street, on Manhattan's Upper West Side. Although less elegant than the Upper East Side where they initially lived, it was a peaceful, intellectual area owing to its proximity to Columbia University. Their apartment had none of the stylishness of their Paris home, which Svetlana Alexeïeff remembered with wonder as a place that was "unique in the world" with its immaculate white walls.[21] When André Schiffrin commented on the photographs of his new apartment in New York, what he remembered most was its "poor, sad"[22] state.

The other priority was finding work, as Jacques Schiffrin wrote to Gustavo Gili on October 8, 1941: "Finding work here is not easy! . . . And sometimes we wonder what will become of us a short time from now. . . . It isn't easy for a foreigner to

find work. But I must, and (for now!) I'm not giving up hope."
Jacques's brother Simon had already left New York after trying,
and failing, to find work for six months. He went to California,
to Hollywood, where, according to Jacques, it wasn't "easy to find
work either."[23] Jacques's difficult employment situation lasted a
long time. In a letter to André Gide dated April 22, 1942, Schiffrin said he was "still unemployed."[24]

Initially, it was thanks to Simone that the family made ends
meet. Simone Schiffrin began working in New York by making "decorations for dresses and hats: brooches, pins, buttons,
etc., etc., etc., that she 'sculpted' out of a kind of plaster and then
painted."[25] Simone was very successful with this work, which
she did from home, selling to the most important couturiers
in the city, to the great pride of her husband, who also lent her
a hand. Unable to find work in publishing, he helped his wife
as a jewelry maker, helping make brooches and other items.
Jacques Schiffrin had left the *Éditions de la Pléiade* far behind,
even though he was continuing to make beautiful things, but
as he wrote to Gide, "what is essential is to earn my bread and
butter."[26] Simone's business was so successful that it soon grew,
and she was selling her buttons to customers in Beverly Hills.[27]
While Jacques and Simone were working, André was sent to
board in a French school an hour away, in New Jersey, and saw
his parents only on weekends.

A few years later, in 1945, Simone wrote a highly emotional
letter to her sister, Jacqueline, who had remained in France,
telling her about their first few months in New York. What
stands out is her sense of guilt at having "fled," which she felt
seemed cowardly compared with the situation of others who had
remained in the eye of the storm. She mentions "this horrible
feeling that we fled, escaped the danger, while leaving everyone
else prey to God knows what abominable destiny." And then,

in this most intimate of letters between sisters, we can see how truly painful the family's initial time in New York was: "I was terribly unhappy and Yacha [Jacques][28] was as well—I'm talking about our life in N.Y.: It was very hard. . . . We had $400, which is nothing."[29]

The family's unhappiness seemed to stem from a combination of their guilt over leaving, their nostalgia for their former world—André Schiffrin spoke of "Paradise Lost"—and their difficulty in building a new life in such a big city. In the same letter to her sister, Simone wrote about her first steps in building a business that allowed her family to overcome some of their financial worries:

> I was extraordinarily lucky to earn $100 by sewing, then, because I needed buttons for the suit I'd made, I managed to sell the buttons that Yacha [Jacques] and I made to all the most important fashion houses in New York. Yacha was very brave; his health has been totally ruined by the pneumonia he caught while he was a soldier and which has left him with a deadly, untreatable form of emphysema; he agreed to become a manual worker, and for twelve hours a day, he has his hands covered in plaster to fill the orders I got by running to the 'couturiers' all over the city from morning to night. I very quickly had eight or ten workers, and all from my apartment.[30]

Such words depict a united couple facing their difficulties, and they convey praise for Jacques's courage, despite an illness that had persisted since the start of the war. However, working together could not heal the suffering Simone described, a psychological anguish that manifested itself physically: "Emotionally, we've both been very bad. I got very sick, unable to sleep at all and constantly worried." And later, Simone speaks of an "anguish that cannot be calmed."

In a personal message to Jacques, Simone went into detail about her life as an insomniac, the daily suffering she observed with a certain amused distance:

> So, between three in the morning and midnight tonight, I listened to the radio forty-seven times, lit, smoked and put out twenty-nine cigarettes, ate "a little something" an excessive number of times, and realized that day had followed night because my terrifying amount of energy had disappeared and made way for a no less terrifying desire to sleep. . . . This said, in twenty-one hours of no sleeping and not doing anything, the house is so clean it is sickening.[31]

This was how Simone Schiffrin spent her days when she wasn't working: suffering boredom and insomnia that never left her. But her insomnia was also the spur that urged her to work and seemed to lessen her suffering. Simone got up at five thirty and never went to bed "before two o'clock".[32]

Simone could not sleep, and, as for Jacques, on April 22, 1942, he described his weariness in a letter to Gide: "I'm still unemployed, which leaves me very demoralized. So tired I could drop. Coughing more than ever, and smoking constantly, in despair and saddened, with the feeling that my life is over and that I am pointlessly dragging myself around while waiting to die."[33] And on August 1, 1942, nearly a year after his arrival, he again confided to Gide: "I am sad, so sad I could die. I don't know how to laugh anymore." Nevertheless, the family had known worse, as he admitted to Gide: "Still, less anguished than when we were in Saint-Tropez".[34]

Perhaps, and most importantly, the Schiffrins were not alone in New York. They were joined by others who had fled Europe and settled in New York. For example, Schiffrin described a meeting with Kurt Wolff in a letter to Gili dated October 8, 1941: "There are many German publishers. Among others, I met Kurt Wolff, a charming man with whom I talked a lot about you. He doesn't know what he is going to be able to do either."[35]

Thus, Jacques Schiffrin was not the only highly qualified European unable to find a way to use his talent or passion in New York during the war. In France, Jacques Schiffrin was considered one of the best publishers in the country. The same applied to Kurt Wolff in Germany. So why should they not succeed together in New York? Especially since publishing was flourishing.

JACQUES SCHIFFRIN & CO. PUBLISHERS: THE EARLY DAYS

During the Second World War, New York was a safe haven for many intellectuals forced to flee Europe and became an important international publishing and cultural center. If certain publishers in Paris continued to publish only those books authorized by the Nazis, others preferred to cross the Atlantic to continue their work. In New York, nearly 250 books were published in French between 1941 and 1944.[36] The vitality of Francophone literature in New York during the war was primarily a result of the high demand created by the French immigrant population.

Several publishing houses were created between the Hudson and East Rivers. The *Éditions de la Maison française* was the most prominent, linked to the Bookstore of the Maison française, then located at Rockefeller Plaza. The *Éditions de la Maison française* published the greatest names in Francophone literature, most of whom were exiles in the United States during the war, including Antoine de Saint-Exupéry, André Maurois, Jacques

Maritain, and Jules Romains. Many of these works examined the situation in France under Nazi occupation, and no translations were listed in the catalog of the *Maison française*.[37] At the same time, the bookstore Brentano's, which had opened in New York at the end of the nineteenth century and had had a location in Paris for several decades, expanded into publishing and launched the publication of a series of French books under the direction of a well-known Parisian lawyer, Robert Tenger. Brentano's catalog contained certain "classics" from among the exiles whose works were also published by the *Maison française*, such as Maurois and Saint-Exupéry. Brentano's had several remarkable successes, obtaining permission from André Breton to publish the only two books he brought out in the United States: *Arcane 17* and *Le Surréalisme et la peinture* (*Surrealism and Painting*). The poet Saint-John Perse and even the Hegelian philosopher Alexandre Koyré enriched Robert Tenger's list.[38] The *Éditions de la Maison française* and Brentano's dominated the Francophone book market in New York. Simultaneously, several other smaller publishing houses were trying to expand, including *Éditions Didier*, which published only about twenty works during the war, most notably the memoirs of Pierre Mendès France.[39] Music lovers could find pleasure in works published by France Music, while poetry enthusiasts enjoyed the works published by *Hémisphères*.[40] One new publisher bore the name of its founder: Jacques Schiffrin & Co.

Schiffrin's early days in the publishing business in New York were challenging. He had initially attempted to re-launch his *Pléiade* collection, explaining to Gide in August 1942,

> I almost managed to reconstruct the *Pléiade* here. But the Gallimards imposed so many conditions that I didn't want to accept. (In short: In addition to a commission on everything I published

here, which was actually quite reasonable, they proposed reducing my royalties in France by two-thirds. That is all fairly theoretical, in fact, since I'm not getting any royalties at the moment—and when and how would I get them? But I found the idea of "punishing me" incredible when I was going to bring them business in which they risked nothing: no capital, no work, no risk whatsoever, an enterprise that would not in any way compete with them, so I turned it down.)[41]

Jacques Schiffrin wished to publish the *Pléiade* editions from New York with capital that did not come from Gallimard. To do this, he would have to get Gallimard's permission for the distribution of works from the collection he had founded in the United States. On October 31, 1941, almost one year to the day after writing the letter that removed the *Pléiade* from its founder, Gaston Gallimard again wrote to Jacques Schiffrin:

> We are proposing certain conditions that seem fair to us: We will grant you or a company you manage the exclusive right to publish and sell works in America, in French, from our collection *Bibliothèque de la Pléiade*, that have been published to date, but without allowing you to undertake the publication of new works in the same collection; however, you would be able to publish new works that I publish myself in this collection as and when they are published in France by filing for the copyright on those titles.
>
> We will receive 4 percent on the sale price of the works you publish, on condition that for the entire period you sell in America, the percentage that we currently owe you would be reduced from 3 percent to 1 percent, and no royalties would be payable to you at all for any books sold in America by your company.[42]

Gaston Gallimard's letter reveals that Jacques Schiffrin had the opportunity of resuming work in New York by continuing his development of the *Pléiade*. However, the conditions imposed were not acceptable to Schiffrin, who wished to continue the *Pléiade* in New York with his own capital, and without links to Gallimard. Schiffrin still had royalties owed to him for works published in the *Pléiade* collection in Paris—though he didn't know how or when he would receive them—and refused to accept them being reduced if he distributed works in the United States. So Schiffrin refused the offer, not wishing to appear to be the American pawn of the Gallimard publishing house, taking both financial and professional risks himself while Gallimard invested nothing in the project.

André Gide was very sorry to see this opportunity slip by and wrote to Jacques Schiffrin on September 5, 1942, expressing his indignation over Gallimard's attitude and saying he would send the last letter Schiffrin had received from Gallimard to their mutual friend, Roger Martin du Gard:

> I'm going to send him your letter ("a copy"); he will no doubt be as indignant as I am at the Gallimard brothers' unenthusiastic agreement to the idea of the *Pléiade* project in the USA; and I so wished it would happen! I deeply regret not having been consulted about it or with them when they sent their reply. . . . What an admirable, once-in-a-lifetime opportunity they have passed up![43]

Thus, Jacques Schiffrin's first attempt at launching himself in the New York publishing world ended in failure.[44]

However, this initial disappointment did not discourage Jacques Schiffrin from pursuing his desire to return to publishing, and, in the summer of 1942, Jacques obtained his first contract, working for Brentano's. In a letter dated August 2, 1942, to

his close friend Boris Souvarine (Russian by birth but a naturalized French citizen who was also in exile in the United States),
Schiffrin exclaimed, "I've just joined Brentano's as a member
of the French publications staff. It's not very well paid but I'm
delighted."[45] However, Schiffrin's time at Brentano's would be
brief. There was little to do, as Robert Tenger was taking care of
almost everything, and Schiffrin also had other projects in mind.
The liberation of North Africa after November 1942, as a result
of the success of the Anglo-American Operation Torch, brought
new possibilities.[46] This reversal of fortune during the war facili-
tated the links and exchange of manuscripts between the newly
free North Africa and the United States. Schiffrin could now
publish books in New York written by French writers and sent to
him via French North Africa.

In 1943, Jacques Schiffrin & Co. was born. Schiffrin launched
his company with two other associates, both French immigrants who loved literature and were passionate experts on the
history of art: Béatrice Laval and André Rouchaud. But it was
Jacques Schiffrin who carried the publishing house, reading and
re-reading, questioning, critiquing, and developing the works he
considered publishing.

In September 1943, Jacques Schiffrin announced the major
change in his life to André Gide: "Things are going on that will
change everything for me: As I said in my telegram (did you
get it?), I've just started a publishing house (bearing my name
+ & Co.)"[47]

In his autobiography, André Schiffrin talks about his father's
first publishing enterprise, describing it as a political act aimed
in part at supporting the Resistance. Certain works published by
this "very small publishing house"[48] were evidence of this: Louis
Aragon's war poems, as well as two other great works of resistance: *Les Silences de la mer* (sic) (*The Silence of the Sea*), the author

of which was unknown to Schiffrin at the time,[49] and *L'Armée des ombres* (*The Army of Shadows*) by Joseph Kessel.[50] These books were intended for the French-speaking public, mainly those in exile in New York. However, as André Schiffrin emphasized, to Americans, and particularly to New Yorkers, "the books played a symbolic role in showing that there was more to France than Vichy's cowardice and complicity."[51]

As mentioned, for Schiffrin, publishing during the Second World War was not simply a literary activity; books were "weapons"[52] of culture in a global conflict. The correspondence between Schiffrin and Gide, one of the main authors Schiffrin would publish in his new publishing house, bears witness to the strategies the publisher and author put into action to receive manuscripts that embodied the spirit of resistance.

From September 1943 onward, Schiffrin asked Gide to send him his *Interviews imaginaires* (*Imaginary Interviews*) and his translation of *Hamlet*. Schiffrin aspired to launch his new collection with the publication of Gide's *Imaginary Interviews*. This project had an important symbolic meaning to Schiffrin, who had launched his *Éditions de la Pléiade* in Paris twenty years earlier by publishing Pushkin's *Queen of Spades* with the collaboration of André Gide.[53] Moreover, in addition to the translation of *Hamlet*, Schiffrin asked Gide to send him "anything else you want to give me."[54]

Gide was delighted with his friend's new project. In September 1943, he told Schiffrin he was ready to send his translation of *Hamlet* from Rabat via Algiers, where he had left the manuscript. Gide even offered Schiffrin his most recent unpublished works:

I can send you an important text (*Pages de Journal 1939–1942*), which I've just sent to London where it will come out as the second *Cahier du Silence* [*Notebook of Silence*]. I specified to that publisher that I was licensing them the rights for only a limited edition (five thousand at most) and did not exclude any other publication of this text in America, France or any other country; so you could also publish it.[55]

Gide thought he could send Schiffrin his *Pages de Journal* via England, which, along with North Africa, was the best channel for Schiffrin and the New York publishing community to receive European works. Ultimately, Jacques Schiffrin & Co. became the leading publisher of Francophone literature in the United States during World War II and made Schiffrin an essential go-between for European literature.

Schiffrin was the official publisher of Gide's works in the United States, as he confirmed in a letter in September 1943: "I want you to know that, here, I am your publisher. Need I say that from every point of view, I will do better for you than anyone else?"[56] In November 1943, Schiffrin could proudly tell his friend that his *Interviews imaginaires*, first published in *Le Figaro*, were in production. The forthcoming publication aroused interest in Gide's works in the United States, as Schiffrin told him at the beginning of November 1943:

> Everyone is excited about the publication of your *Interviews*, both French and Americans alike, with "*Hénorme*" [enormous][57] anticipation. You would never believe it—so I must tell you—how many people are eager to read you. I am preparing for the *Interviews* to be a great event. Everyone wants the *Journal* ("Pléiade") and there are none left. I want to speak to you about that as well and will as soon as I can.[58]

Schiffrin's publication of major contemporary works by André Gide was greeted with great interest by New York's intellectual community, most especially by recent French immigrants. Jacques Schiffrin & Co. also reached the West Coast. While Simone Schiffrin's buttons were being delivered to Beverly Hills boutiques, Jacques's books were going to bookstores in California. In a letter to Jacques Schiffrin & Co., Nadia Boulanger, the great French musician who was in exile in Santa Barbara during the war, wrote,

Dear Sir,

When I learned you were going to publish books here—I can't tell you the joy I felt—your work is so very important—today more than ever—and even more generally—for only men of your taste can ensure high quality, without which nothing is of any value.

If you are an ironic person, my effusion will make you smile—but I prefer to take that chance, a slight one at that, since I wish to thank you personally, in all sincerity.

Nadia Boulanger[59]

Many French immigrants had been in the United States for two or three years and were eager for news from their country. Moreover, they considered that Jacques Schiffrin's publication of French works provided an opportunity to remain connected to the land of their birth. In addition, as Nadia Boulanger said, Schiffrin's publishing house was a symbolic act of resistance in itself, an act of high quality and taste, through literature, opposed to the barbarity in the world.

On December 9, 1943, Gide wrote to Schiffrin to discuss their projects:

Determined to support your new firm in the best and friendliest way possible, I am sending you, in a secure manner, the text of the *Journal* (September '39–January '42), which I already sent with the

Cahiers du silence[60] in London. The sequel to this *Journal* can be sent only at a later date, for personal reasons. But you will also receive my translation of *Hamlet* (I'm just finishing up the final touches); delighted about your plan to bring out this edition with the English text opposite. The *Anthologie* will follow; I still haven't completed the very important preface. Regarding a reprint of my *Journal* (*Pléiade*), I would gladly give my consent, but there is the question of Gallimard: We'll try to obtain some agreement, but that will also depend on how events play out. Let's come back to that.[61]

Thus, the *Pages de Journal* were coming via London and *Hamlet* via North Africa (Algeria, then Morocco); the sequel to the *Journal* and the *Anthologie* would follow; and the publication of the *Journal*, which had initially been part of the *Éditions de la Pléiade*, had to be put on hold pending negotiations with Gallimard, who owned the rights.

In December 1943, Jacques Schiffrin's first book was published in New York: *Interviews imaginaires* by André Gide, accompanied by a text entitled *La Délivrance de Tunis* (*The Liberation of Tunis*), a more journalistic portion of Gide's wartime diaries praising the Allies' success in ending the occupation of the Tunisian capital and condemning Hitler and the Axis powers. The book's cover was green, a contrast to but also a reminder of the pale colors used for the *Éditions de la Pléiade*; on the cover was a large, dark green rectangle with a smaller, light green rectangle within it. Over the light green was written the author's name, ANDRE GIDE, in darker green capital letters, and at the bottom of the lighter rectangle, in a smaller font of the same color, was the name of the publisher: EDITIONS JACQUES SCHIFFRIN. In the center, in white italic font, was the book's title: *Interviews imaginaires*. And so Jacques Schiffrin had published his first book in the United States; nearly three years after being dismissed by Gaston Gallimard, he was once again a publisher.

The book's first page announced the future publications of Jacques Schiffrin & Co. In addition to Gide, three other names appeared: André Breton, Julien Green, and Denis de Rougemont,[62] all exiles in the United States. When it came to choosing which works to publish, Schiffrin leaned toward books written by people who had experienced the war in Europe first hand, like Gide and Vercors, rather than those in exile. Schiffrin was in contact with Breton, the author of the *Manifeste du Surréalisme* (*Manifesto of Surrealism*), but no publication ever materialized. In a letter dated February 29, 1944, to Breton, then living in New York, regarding his *Anthologie de l'humour noir* (*Anthology of Black Humor*), Schiffrin wrote, "Rouchaud[63] no doubt told you what difficulties we are having in obtaining paper and other material. We nevertheless still hope to be your publisher, and as soon as possible. Your devoted Jacques Schiffrin."[64] During the war, a very small organization like Jacques Schiffrin & Co. couldn't find a way around the wartime restrictions on obtaining paper, which occasionally prevented Schiffrin from publishing authors when he wanted to.

As for the possibility of publishing Julien Green, there was a project that dated back to May 1942: "Publishing the third volume of my *Journal* here would be the easiest thing in the world to justify because it would not be possible in France at present," Green wrote. And in the same letter: "As soon as you know for sure that you can publish my book, let me know."[65]

In July, the same project was again discussed in a letter from Green to Schiffrin:

> I am working a lot, work for me is a kind of drug that helps a little to forget the sadness we all feel. I'm making progress on my

translation of Péguy, as well as my journal. The typed copy of the journal currently has one hundred and forty pages, which isn't enough for a book, but I think I'll manage to get it to two hundred pages before the winter. For now, if you agree, we can continue our discussion of last April, for I am thinking about our publishing project a great deal.[66]

Ultimately, Green would never publish his *Journal*, either in part or as a complete work, with Jacques Schiffrin & Co. Not enough paper? Not enough time or money? The publisher's preference for books written in Europe? Undoubtedly a combination of all of the above.

The problem of obtaining paper was also mentioned in a letter dated March 7, 1944, from the Swiss writer Denis de Rougemont, whose *Les Personnes du drame* Schiffrin had planned to publish: "Rouchaud told me about your current list and your difficulty in obtaining paper. With my usual insight, I'm deducing that you won't be able to publish my book for a long time."[67]

Despite the shortage of paper owing to wartime rationing, by the end of 1943, Jacques Schiffrin's new publishing house was expanding. On December 27, Schiffrin received a letter from Gide giving him full rights to the translation of his works throughout North and South America. At about the same time, in January 1944, Schiffrin published Gide's *Cahiers du silence* and Vercors's *Les Silences de la mer* (sic), which he had received via London. Vercors's identity was, at this point, still a mystery to Gide and Schiffrin. Gide was certain that Vercors was a writer named Lacretelle, whereas Schiffrin thought it was a work by Sartre.[68]

Schiffrin's publishing strategy could be quite diversified, especially where the translation of Gide's *Hamlet* was concerned. Schiffrin wanted to publish two editions: "a 'popular' one that could easily be bought by everyone (and especially by universities, colleges and libraries) and a deluxe edition: limited print run, very luxurious."[69] However, communication between Gide and Schiffrin was extremely difficult; letters did not always reach them, and the war caused many delays. So Schiffrin did what he could. In February 1944, he entrusted his brother Simon, who was traveling to Algiers, with a letter to André Gide that summarized their agreement.[70] When he returned, Simon brought with him some texts from Gide, including a few additional pages from the *Journal*.[71]

This was how publishers and authors were forced to communicate between continents during the war. Schiffrin also did everything he could to pay Gide, who was then based in Morocco. First and foremost, he used people who were traveling, like the Surrealist poet Philippe Soupault, whom Schiffrin gave $500 to pass on to Gide. He also asked Gide to open an account with the State Bank of Morocco in Fez so he could deposit money from New York.[72] However, Gide preferred that Schiffrin open an account in his name in New York, which would allow him to have a "good reserve of dollars in America." A few years later, in 1948, Gide would buy himself an American car with that money, a blue DeSoto.[73]

By the end of 1943, after finally launching his career as a New York publisher, Jacques Schiffrin found his morale much improved. As he wrote to Gide on December 17, "We are doing as well as possible".[74]

The numerous colloquialisms he used in his correspondence are evidence of his progress in English. Jacques Schiffrin was gradually integrating himself into life in New York, and a world that might have appeared hostile when he first arrived no longer felt so. Needless to say, challenges remained: His company remained very small, and he was working almost alone from the small apartment on the Upper East Side where he had recently moved, with only André Rouchaud and Béatrice Laval helping him. Most importantly, his new enterprise did not meet his family's needs. As André Schiffrin wrote, "The number of copies that my father was able to sell was tiny, certainly not enough to live on."[75] Though not enough to support his family, it was more than sufficient to make his name in the New York publishing world. And it was certainly enough to join Pantheon Books, one of the boldest publishing ventures in twentieth-century America, launched a few years before by Kurt Wolff, the German publisher in exile.

PANTHEON BOOKS

Jacques Schiffrin and Kurt Wolff certainly knew of each other in Europe, and once in New York, they saw each other via various shared artistic and literary circles. In the first letter Schiffrin sent from America to Gustavo Gili, in Barcelona, in October 1941, he wrote of having met Kurt Wolff, "a charming man."[76] According to his daughter Svetlana, they first met at the home of the Russian engraver Alexandre Alexeïeff.[77] Over a long, pleasant dinner, the two publishers got to know each other, spoke French with their host, and discussed the Europe they had left and their plans for life in America. Kurt's wife, Helen, got to know Simone Schiffrin through Claire Parker, Alexeïeff's partner. This meeting was the beginning of the two men's relationship, although they did not immediately form a partnership.

Jacques Schiffrin had initially been living on the Upper West Side, an area where intellectual refugees of German Jewish descent had primarily settled.[78] Schiffrin, who spoke several languages, did not fit the typical mold of a Frenchman in exile, a fact he himself recognized.[79] This could explain why Schiffrin never completely connected with the French publishing houses that were already well established in Manhattan. Instead, Jacques Schiffrin would go into business with someone like himself, someone who had traveled virtually the same route: Kurt Wolff.

Kurt Wolff and Jacques Schiffrin were part of the same generation. Wolff[80] was born into a German Jewish family in Bonn in 1887. His father was a university professor and his mother a conductor. He studied at prestigious German universities in Bonn, Munich, Marburg, and Leipzig before launching his own publishing house in 1913: *Kurt Wolff Verlag.* As the publisher of Franz Kafka, among other notable writers, Wolff rapidly became recognized as one the most important German publishers. However, with the rise of anti-Semitism and the Nazi Party, Wolff was forced to leave Germany. At the beginning of the 1930s, he went to England and then Italy, and then to Nice with his second wife, Helen, and their son, Christian. From France, thanks to Varian Fry's network, he escaped Europe and arrived in New York in 1941, a few months before Jacques Schiffrin. From then on, like so many other exiles, Wolff began looking for work. He spent his days at the New York Public Library, trying to identify possible gaps in the American publishing market and what German books were unavailable in English.

In 1942, Wolff decided to launch his own publishing house: Pantheon Books. Because he was a German national, the American authorities considered Wolff a potentially dangerous person. Thus, although he was Jewish and a refugee, he could not give his own name to the publishing house he had founded or even legally register it himself. One of his old friends from Munich, Curt von Faber du Faur, was also in New York. Du Faur was eclectic in his pursuits: an antiques dealer, collector, professor, and art critic. Along with his son-in-law, Kyrill Schabert, du Faur invested the $7,500 Wolff needed to establish his publishing house. It was agreed that until the company turned a profit, Kurt Wolff would not take a salary. The very first employee of Pantheon Books was Wolfgang Sauerlander, who had also fled Nazi Germany. Before becoming a key figure in the company, Sauerlander began his stint at Pantheon by addressing and mailing envelopes. The enterprise itself began modestly, being run out of Wolff's apartment in Washington Square.

Kurt Wolff's journey had been similar to Jacques Schiffrin's,[81] and their shared experience of being in exile brought the two men closer. Like Schiffrin, Wolff had faced serious difficulties during his first months in New York, which he described in his memories of his early days in America: "I was about fifty, and it is very difficult to adapt to a foreign country if you cannot master the language. Convincing authors was not easy. My American publishing career did not really begin until I realized, 'You are in a country where you could become a pioneer.'"[82]

Jacques Schiffrin had encountered the same problem when he first arrived in New York: being over fifty and forced to start again, learn a new language, and make a place for himself in a new publishing culture. Wolff and Schiffrin also shared the same passions: literature and a kind of publishing that refused to sacrifice quality for profit or the ideal of a beautiful object on the altar of consumerism. This idea was expressed in a letter from Helen Wolff to the historian Laura Fermi:

> When I think back on those years, it seems difficult to answer your question about the thinking in founding a publishing house in America. Thinking itself was a luxury at the time. For both of them, it was a question of survival. For both of them publishing was their profession. No American publishing offered them the opportunity of using their experience. They had no choice but to

start their own—European methods were introduced not by special planning but because of previous experience. They consisted mainly in the fundamental approach, which was the same for Kurt Wolff and Jacques Schiffrin: that a publishing house had to have a physiognomy, that is should reflect the taste of the publishers, and that it should not publish indiscriminately whatever promised to sell. Books were not considered merchandise but objects of permanent value, an attitude that dictated particular care in their production.[83]

In 1944, these two publishers, well known for their passion for literature, elegance, and talent, transformed their close relationship into a common destiny when Jacques Schiffrin joined Pantheon Books.

Pantheon Books would become a transit point, a bridge between Europe and the United States. The publishing house's maxim declared its literary agenda: "Classics that are modern, Moderns that are classic." Even though Pantheon had been founded in 1942, when Jacques Schiffrin was still helping his wife with her textile business, it was not until 1943 that it published its first book: *Basic Verities: Poetry and Prose* by Charles Péguy (1873–1914), translated by Julien Green and his sister Anne Green. To Wolff, it was important to launch his new enterprise by publishing an author like Péguy, who personified spiritual strength and patriotism at a time when France was experiencing defeat and humiliation. It seems likely that Jacques Schiffrin would have been consulted on such a project, as Jacques Schiffrin & Co. had originally intended to publish the work, and Wolff and Schiffrin were drawn to the same authors.

After the publication of the first dozen or so books—including volumes of poetry, books on art, history, and philosophy, and fictional works—Pantheon was on the map in New York publishing, and, in 1944, looking to expand, Kurt Wolff asked Jacques Schiffrin to join his office at 41 Washington Square. In addition to his responsibilities for producing graphics and general editing duties, Schiffrin was put in charge of a specific collection: the French Pantheon Book. Pantheon's leading role in bringing European works to the United States was strengthened by the numerous bilingual editions Pantheon published, including, in French, Péguy and Claudel, and, in German, the poetry of Stefan George.

Jacques Schiffrin's plan to bring out a bilingual edition of *Hamlet*, with a French translation by André Gide, fit perfectly with Pantheon's editorial practices. Moreover, the works on art that Pantheon published from 1943 onward evoked a world that Schiffrin knew well. The books Kurt Wolff brought out on Daumier, Maillol, and Pissarro appealed to Jacques Schiffrin's education in art history with Bernard Berenson and in art publishing with Henri Piazza.

Schiffrin was fully committed to his new publishing house, working with Wolff on new ventures for Pantheon, and using his network and catalog to provide the house with new projects. Unsurprisingly, André Gide followed his friend and would be published by Pantheon Books in the United States from that point on.

Pantheon's catalog illustrated the editorial choices of Wolff and Schiffrin.[84] In 1944, their list contained a new collection: "The French Pantheon, a new series under the direction of Jacques Schiffrin, publishes books in French by outstanding contemporary French authors." This catalog included authors with whom Schiffrin had been in contact when he started Jacques Schiffrin & Co. Pantheon published André Gide's *Journal (1939–42)*, which he had promised to Schiffrin, while his *Interviews imaginaires*, which had sold five thousand copies, was republished by the two men from Washington Square.[85] Faithful to his recipe for success, Schiffrin used a format similar to the one he had used for the *Pléiade*, as he wrote in a letter to Gide in December 1944: "cloth instead of leather, and naturally on 'Bible paper,'[86] but the same format, same spine, same jacket, etc. Very attractive."[87]

The composer Darius Milhaud, who was then in California, thanked Schiffrin for sending him a copy of Gide's *Journal (1939–1942)*, remarking on the similarity between its format and that of books published in the *Éditions de la Pléiade*: "You have given us enormous pleasure by sending Gide's *Journal* in this edition, which reminds us of the *Pléiade*."[88] Denis de Rougemont also published *Les Personnes du drame* in French with Pantheon in October 1944 under Jacques Schiffrin's direction. *Les Silences de la mer* (sic), finally attributed to Vercors, and Joseph Kessel's *L'Armée des ombres* were also on Pantheon's list. These two last works dealt directly and powerfully with the subject of resistance and of the world of silence and shadows that had spread throughout Europe and echoed in the literature of the time.

In his role as publisher, Schiffrin was one of the people who showed the community of European immigrants in America that there was still hope. By doing so, he was, in his own way, participating in the Resistance. Yet, his books were also aimed at the cultured American public. The *New York Times* considered *L'Armée des ombres* "one of the most horrific and moving books of our era."[89] In 1945 and 1946, the French Pantheon Books collection would continue to publish outstanding works: Vercors's *La Marche à l'Étoile* (*The Guiding Star*), the bilingual version of *Hamlet* with Gide's translation, and Gide's *Thésée* (*Theseus*). In July 1946, Schiffrin also published a work in New York that was causing a sensation in France: *L'Étranger* (*The Stranger*) by Albert Camus.

The contract between Jacques Schiffrin and Albert Camus reflected how problematic it was for Pantheon to acquire rights for the books it published. In a letter to Schiffrin dated May 15, 1946, Camus discussed the legal terms and conditions for Pantheon to obtain rights to *The Stranger*. Even though Gallimard was publishing the book, they did not own the exclusive rights in the Western Hemisphere; that is, in North and South America. Schiffrin was quick to exploit this geographical loophole to negotiate with Camus: "Through this letter, you confirm that you are entirely free to personally negotiate the assignment of rights of the book involved in this agreement and you guarantee that no complaint can be directed against us from the *Librairie Gallimard*, who owns the copyright of this work."[90] Camus would receive 8 percent of the retail price of each copy sold and an advance of $300. And with those terms, Schiffrin became the American publisher of *The Stranger*, which he published in French.

Quality was the essential element in the editorial choices of Kurt Wolff and Jacques Schiffrin. Pantheon Books published works by Tolstoy, Hermann Broch's *Les Somnambules* (*The Sleepwalkers*), Georges Bernanos's *Lettre aux Anglais* (*Plea for Liberty*), Grimms' *Fairy Tales*—which was hugely successful, selling nearly twenty-five thousand copies—and *Les Mille et une nuits* (*The Thousand and One Nights*) illustrated by Marc Chagall, along with works of art history focused on Manet and Degas. Wolff and Schiffrin's decision to publish Bernanos's *Plea for Liberty* (1944) and debut novel *Under the Sun of Satan* (1949) in English was not motivated by "commercial reasons," as Jacques Schiffrin explained to his brother Simon, but because "all of us at Pantheon admire him greatly."[91]

In addition to managing Pantheon, Schiffrin and Wolff were also in charge of the editorial and design policies of the

Bollingen Foundation,[92] as requested by Paul Mellon and Mary Conover Mellon, wealthy American patrons of the arts, who had established the Foundation to publish scholarly books in classical and European culture for an American audience. Later, the Foundation would also publish the works of Jung along with books on Eastern traditions and religion. Additionally, with Bollingen, Wolff and Schiffrin published works on art in the United States, such as Malraux's *Musée imaginaire* (*Imaginary Museum*).

Along with its work at the Bollingen Foundation, Pantheon Books had its sights firmly on Europe. Schiffrin and Wolff published works written in Europe that spoke of Europe, but with the goal of bringing an ethos of quality and a richness of history, as well as doubt and skepticism, to the United States, where a spirit of certainty could reign. By doing so, Pantheon Books fully participated in a transfer of culture, the *translatio studii* that was in play between Europe and the United States during the Second World War.

At Pantheon Books, Jacques Schiffrin became a major publisher again. His work was admired, and Pantheon became one of the best-known publishing houses in New York. The books published by Kurt Wolff and Jacques Schiffrin received extremely favorable reviews in the New York press. But Jacques Schiffrin also rediscovered a specific atmosphere at Pantheon: a constant exchange of ideas and working with colleagues that his years of a "nomadic existence" had taken away from him. He had loved his work at Schiffrin & Co., but that company was too small to provide him the feeling of embarking on a collective enterprise.

At Pantheon, Schiffrin rubbed shoulders with some of the most important people in New York's literary and cultural worlds. At a party at 41 Washington Square to celebrate Pantheon's birthday, Svetlana Alexeïeff recounts that a very wise,

FIGURE 2.1 Kurt Wolff and Jacques Schiffrin in the Pantheon Books offices in Washington Square, New York.

unpretentious man suddenly came up to her, gave her a kiss, and said she had "all of Russia" in her beautiful eyes.[93] The man was Marc Chagall, who was then in exile in New York.

With his work at Washington Square, Jacques Schiffrin had developed a routine that made his life in exile more acceptable and helped him settle into New York City living. André Schiffrin observed this adjustment:

> Some of the few places in New York where my father found he could feel at home were the little Italian cafés behind Pantheon's offices on Washington Square. These were not the fancy espresso joints of later years, but tiny, barren, working-class storefronts, each with a coffee machine and a few linoleum-covered tables. But they sold very good, very strong espresso and accepted anyone who wanted to join the game of gin rummy that the old Italian immigrants played all day long. I would often find Jacques there, happily playing cards during his lunch break.[94]

The publisher who had traveled such a long and arduous road had now rediscovered the joys of belonging somewhere, as well as a workday that included games and a convivial atmosphere—in short, a real life.

Alongside finding personal satisfaction in his work, Schiffrin's professional life was also expanding and becoming more busy. The Schiffrin family archives contain an exceptional amount of correspondence relating to the history of Pantheon Books.[95] These letters were written between Kurt Wolff and Jacques Schiffrin when they were not in daily contact, mainly during long summer vacations. Dating between 1944 and 1948, the letters are full of technical details, but they also allow for an understanding of Schiffrin's role at the heart of the company, as well as his relationship with Wolff. Jacques Schiffrin's letters, written in French, and Kurt Wolff's replies, written in English, reflect Pantheon's cosmopolitanism, a place where several languages were spoken and writers from all over Europe were discussed. At the same time, Schiffrin now spoke English well enough to receive professional letters in the language of America. Unlike many French immigrants, Schiffrin made the effort to learn the language of his new home, taking private lessons with an English teacher.[96]

Schiffrin normally spent his summer vacations in upstate New York, where he could rest. His letters to Wolff describe his vacations but mainly discuss publishing issues. Schiffrin suggested illustrations for the covers of certain books, like *The Romance of Tristan and Isolde*, for which he created a rough sketch that he sent to Wolff on July 9, 1945. He also kept Wolff informed of his recent correspondence with Gide: "Received a letter from Gide. We can go ahead with *Thésée*. Let's talk about that when I get back." The publishers also discussed the size and type of font to use for back covers and congratulated each other on their various successes.

These letters, written during the summer, also show signs of the lethargy and boredom that Jacques Schiffrin felt when he was not working, forced to spend long weeks in a rest home intended to treat his respiratory problems. In 1946, Schiffrin wrote a letter to Kurt Wolff that opened with a quote from Baudelaire: " 'It is necessary to work, at least out of despair, since when all is said and done, working is less boring than enjoying oneself.' And here—neither work nor amusement. Just boredom. Boredom that I try to overcome with food and sleep."

However, nothing prevented the two friends from discussing their current problems, one of which was obtaining paper, which was still being rationed. In a letter from July 26, 1946, Schiffrin wrote to Wolff about the trouble of obtaining paper,

but its final lines sum up their correspondence, one characterized by eclectic professional questions and personal news
freely exchanged:

> So what are your thoughts on the subject of a book illustrated
> by the French painter? Did you give up on the whole idea? And
> what about the new illustrations for the Selma Lager[97]; did
> you get anything from your German painter? And what about
> the African stories? . . . Nothing exciting my end—bored stiff.
> Warmest wishes.

Sometimes, as in this letter from July 1948, Schiffrin gave his
literary critique of a work:

> I've almost finished Troyat's book *Tant que la Terre durera* [*While
> the Earth Endures*]: It isn't bad. Talented, but not an ounce of
> genius. And it hardly deals with anything that concerns man today.
> It's as if a contemporary painter was painting like a Veronese or
> Rubens. But I didn't think you were planning to publish this book
> at Pantheon, were you?

And in the same letter, as an afterthought: "Did you hear that
Bernanos died? He wasn't even old: only sixty." Jacques Schiffrin
was then fifty-six.

Each of these letters contains rich details on specific aspects
of Pantheon Books. They reveal Schiffrin to be a man fully
involved in the various stages of decision-making at Pantheon.
His influence reached far beyond the collection of French books,
and he gave his opinion on every subject. His mastery of English
bears witness to an authentic effort at integrating into American life and publishing. Most importantly, Schiffrin and Wolff
shared a similar vision and developed a true friendship.

Schiffrin's exchange of letters with Kurt Wolff coincided with correspondence between Schiffrin and Pantheon's first employee, Wolfgang Sauerlander.[98] Along with Wolff and Schiffrin, Sauerlander was one of the key figures at Pantheon. As in his correspondence with Wolff, Schiffrin and Sauerlander discussed such details as the color of book jackets, corrections, edits, and font choices. But in this relationship, it was Jacques Schiffrin who led and dominated the exchanges, questioning and criticizing his colleague. In a letter dated July 17, 1948, he candidly writes, "You've made a mistake; send me the correct statement." And he did not hesitate to get annoyed, as is evident in a letter dated July 30, 1948, in which he loses his temper: "WOLFGANG! Where did you get the stupid idea to publish Martin's illustrations and the subtitles by A. B.?!" Conversely, Sauerlander asked Schiffrin to act as an arbiter, deciding among several options. Schiffrin seems to have sometimes behaved so harshly toward his employee that, in a letter dated August 18, he felt the need to explain himself: "I'm not impatient with you and I certainly don't think you are 'stupider than the average person.'"

In August 1949, Schiffrin requested Sauerlander's help. He asked his employee to take notes from the Encyclopedia Britannica on the history of the twelve months of the year. Schiffrin wanted to offer a gift to Simon & Schuster, the publishing house they considered a rival but with whom the Pantheon publishers were on very good terms: He called it a "juvenile calendar." And in Jacques Schiffrin's personal papers, there are, in fact, notes about the juvenile calendar he was preparing in the summer of 1949.[99]

Along with the calendar, Schiffrin also seemed to be preparing a collection of jokes.[100] These jokes tended to return to the world of Eastern Europe:

Two Hungarians, both former capitalists, meet in Budapest after the Communist Revolution:
>   —How are you?
>   —Fine, and you?
>   —All right. What are you doing in Budapest?
>   —I'm working for the new government.
>   —Me too; which department?
>   —The police!
>   —That's too funny; me too!
>   —And what do you think of the new government?
>   —The same as you, I guess.
>   —In that case, I'm going to have to arrest you.[101]

It is not known for whom Jacques Schiffrin's dozens of hand-written jokes were intended. They do, however, demonstrate—like the calendar he hoped to create, and his new responsibilities at Pantheon—that Schiffrin was beginning to enjoy life again. He had been shunted back and forth; subjected to bureaucratic red tape, the war, and concern over his fate; and had lost the desire to laugh; but he was now regaining some control over his life. He was involved in many activities, had found his place professionally, and, at the same time, had allowed himself pleasures that would have seemed impossible in his early days in New York.

As a Frenchman in exile, born in the Russian Empire, working alongside a German, and now speaking fluent English, Schiffrin occupied a distinct place in the New York publishing world. He was a go-between in many ways, allowing American readers to discover great French authors such as Gide and Vercors and important Russian artists such as Alexeïeff and Chagall, as well as other authors and thinkers, like Jacques Maritain and Denis de Rougemont. His position at the center of Pantheon Books placed him at the crossroads of several networks that allowed him to be in contact with publishing houses around the world, as well as with authors and intellectuals with whom he maintained relationships in Europe and New York and the European community in exile in the United States.

JACQUES SCHIFFRIN AT THE CROSSROADS OF MANY WORLDS

If the situation of exile contributes to confining an individual, causing him to lose sight of who he is and lose his bearings to the extent that he can no longer find himself, it can also allow the uprooted man to rise. Thus from Rio de Janeiro to Paris, from Montreal to New York, Jacques Schiffrin was in contact with a number of important figures who, for personal and professional reasons, came into contact or corresponded with the man who had become an important New York publisher.

The catalog that Jacques Schiffrin and Kurt Wolff created in New York was of interest well beyond Manhattan. Especially during World War II, with French publishing in crisis and the dispersion of a great number of literary figures around the world, the time was right for the globalization of the publishing market of the United States. New York was at the center of this publishing world, and Jacques Schiffrin played an indispensable role within it.

Since 1943, Schiffrin had been André Gide's legal representative in the Western Hemisphere and had full power over all matters concerning the translation of the author's works. Following the publication of Gide's *Interviews imaginaires* by Jacques Schiffrin & Co., requests to distribute the book flooded the editor's desk. In Rio de Janeiro, a publishing house called

Americ. Edit. wished to buy the rights to Gide's most recent work published in America. Max Fischer, the publisher who contacted Jacques Schiffrin, had formerly worked for Flammarion, the French publishing house, and had gone to Brazil during the war. He contacted Schiffrin on the advice of Philippe Soupault, one of the founders of Surrealism, who told him about the forthcoming publication of the *Interviews imaginaires* in New York. According to Fischer, it would be more advantageous to distribute Gide's works through a publishing house located in South America. But Schiffrin preferred to distribute the work throughout the continent himself and was not prepared to negotiate with Americ. Edit.[102]

Nevertheless, the former Flammarion publisher remained interested in Schiffrin's catalog, mainly those sections of Gide's *Journal* that covered the years 1939 to 1942. He again raised the matter of distributing the French text in South America, Fischer insisting on the comparative advantage of publishing the book in Rio, which would clearly be less difficult than in North America given the expense of importing books during the time. Jacques Schiffrin & Co. would have the exclusive right to sales in North America, and Americ. Edit. would have exclusive rights in South America. Splitting the rights between the two Americas was not a new concept; Fischer confirmed that Robert Tenger, the owner of Brentano's in New York, had proposed the same arrangement for certain works.

In his response, Schiffrin thanked Fischer for his proposal but once again declined, wanting to retain control over the production of all Gide books: "We insist on printing our books here, ourselves. You will understand better than anyone our desire to keep close watch on production, to be able to choose all the elements of a book and to make any little modification during production, etc."[103] This was one of Jacques Schiffrin's characteristics as a publisher: Extremely conscientious, he left nothing to chance and aspired to control every aspect of the publication process if his name was linked to it. Even though Schiffrin was firmly opposed to any other publishing house distributing works in French to which he had the rights, he did leave the door open to a possible translation into Spanish or Portuguese of the previously unpublished sections of Gide's *Journal* that he intended to publish. Ultimately, doing business with Fischer proved to be impossible. Due to a perceived lack of interest among readers of Spanish or Portuguese, Fischer declined to translate Gide's *Interviews imaginaires*.

Nearly two thousand kilometers south of Rio de Janeiro, another Atlantic port was a hub of publishing during World War II. Buenos Aires, the capital of Argentina and a city considered the Paris of South America, had a rich intellectual life, which revolved around individuals such as Jorge Luis Borges, Adolfo Bioy Casares,[104] and Victoria Ocampo, the influential director of the famous literary review *Sur*. Needless to say, it was hardly surprising that Jacques Schiffrin was in contact with this cultural capital of South America.

Founded by Spanish refugees in 1939, the publishing house Emecé Editores was interested in obtaining a certain number of works that Jacques Schiffrin owned the rights to. Once again, Philippe Soupault was the contact who put Schiffrin in touch with Emecé, with a possible translation of Gide's *Interviews imaginaires* under discussion.[105] Victoria Ocampo personally supported Emecé's proposal. Ocampo was of the same generation as Jacques Schiffrin. Born in Buenos Aires, she knew France well, having lived there in the early 1930s, when she was known to be the lover of Pierre Drieu la Rochelle, who would later become a Nazi collaborator. This time, the transaction succeeded, and Schiffrin agreed to license Emecé the rights for a

Spanish translation of *Interviews imaginaires* in exchange for royalties of 10 percent on each copy sold and an advance of $250.

At the beginning of January 1945, Jacques Schiffrin was pleased to receive the first copies of the Spanish translation of Gide's *Interviews imaginaires* (*Reportages imaginarios*). In March 1947, nearly 2,500 copies of the work had been sold throughout South America. A few months later, with Gide's approval, the section of his *Journal* for the years 1939 to 1942 were translated into Spanish by Emecé, with Jacques Schiffrin's permission.[106] The terms and conditions of the contract were the same as for *Interviews imaginaires*. When it came to negotiating contracts, Schiffrin seemed willing to license translation rights to other countries but remained reluctant to license rights for works he published in French, preferring to sell his editions abroad.

Alongside exchanges focused on publishing matters, Schiffrin also corresponded with friends living in Buenos Aires during World War II, like Roger Caillois, formerly of the *NRF*, a member of the French Resistance and the Surrealist group. In March 1944, he wrote to Schiffrin to thank him after receiving the first works published by Jacques Schiffrin & Co., Vercors's *Les Silences de la mer* (sic) and Gide's *Interviews imaginaires*.[107] In addition, Caillois requested Schiffrin's help, asking him if it would be possible to publish extracts from Gide's *Journal* in *Les lettres françaises*, a journal he was publishing from Buenos Aires with Victoria Ocampo's help. After consulting with Schiffrin, Gide accepted the offer, with pleasure.[108] Moreover, as Caillois's mention of Vercors's book illustrates, Schiffrin was more than a simple conduit between Gide and the New World; he was part of a much broader movement spreading French culture across the Atlantic Ocean and throughout both North and South America.

Likewise, Schiffrin was also frequently in contact with the Beauchemin Bookstore in Montreal. In 1945, he received a letter from the store asking to order a number of books from Pantheon. Beauchemin wanted to negotiate the exclusive right to distribute books published in French by Jacques Schiffrin in Canada: Gide's *Journal*, Kessel's *L'Armée des ombres*, and Vercors's *Les Silences de la mer* (sic).[109]

While becoming a fixture in the New York literary scene, Schiffrin maintained contact with numerous European figures through friends and colleagues in the United States who visited the continent. Jacques's brother Simon was frequently in touch with André Gide and also passed on messages on behalf of his brother to French publishers when he visited Paris.[110] And when Kurt Wolff went to Europe just after the end of the war, Schiffrin advised him to visit some friends who had remained in France, like the publisher Henri Filipacchi, whom he described as "very conceited, a great bluffer, [and a] nice young man," and with whom he had worked when founding the *Éditions de la Pléiade*.[111] Moreover, whenever French writers visited the United States, seeing Jacques Schiffrin was almost obligatory. Thus, when Jean-Paul Sartre visited New York at the beginning of 1945, he had dinner with Jacques and Simone. This was also the case for the author of *Le Silence de la mer*, Jean Bruller (a.k.a. Vercors), when he visited New York at the beginning of January 1946.[112] Vercors gave Schiffrin the opportunity to re-immerse himself in the intellectual life of France when he invited him to a party on the Upper East Side at the home of Rudolph Loewenstein, a psychoanalyst in exile who had treated Lacan in Paris in the 1930s. Schiffrin was also a first-hand source of information for Vercors, giving him news of the European writers living in New York.

Of course, there was always his close relationship with André Gide. Schiffrin's prominence as Gide's friend and American publisher reached new heights when, in 1947, Gide won the Nobel Prize in Literature. In many ways, this brought Schiffrin's journey full circle, as the prize, whose founding family had made a fortune in Caspian Sea oil in Baku, was now being awarded to an author so closely associated with him. As the publisher of one of the most important authors in the world, Jacques Schiffrin's place in American and international publishing was now undeniably cemented.

In addition to his continual correspondence with the two most recent French winners of the Nobel Prize in Literature, Roger Martin du Gard, who won in 1937, and Gide, Schiffrin was also in contact with André Malraux, who was appointed Minister of Information after the war by General Charles de Gaulle. At the end of 1945, Malraux contacted Schiffrin, addressing him in a familiar, friendly tone.[113] Malraux was pleased by the close relationship between Alexandre Alexeïeff and Jacques Schiffrin in New York and assured his friend that he was entirely at Schiffrin's disposal if he ever needed help, especially where passports were concerned.

Jacques Schiffrin was also becoming an essential figure for French writers who wanted to be published in New York. When Jean Paulhan, the writer, literary critic, publisher, and director of the *Nouvelle Revue Française* (from 1925 to 1940 and then from 1946 to 1968), wanted to publish his *Entretien sur les faits-divers* (*Interview on various subjects*) in the United States, it was Schiffrin he contacted. On July 21, 1948, Paulhan wrote to him,

> I have a favor to ask of you. Several Americans tell me that my little *Entretien sur les faits-divers* would be much better liked in the United States (where people have, or so I'm told, more of a taste for criticism concerning daily life and condemning everyday illusions . . .) than in France. On the off-chance, I'm entrusting you with my cause (and am sending you a new copy of the book.)[114]

Schiffrin quickly replied "with the eyes of an American publisher."[115] With as much kindness as frankness, he discouraged his friend from trying to break into the American market. To Schiffrin, the book was better suited to the French public than to American readers. In his reply, Paulhan let Schiffrin know that his original idea came from his "advisers," who felt that *Entretien sur les faits-divers* greatly resembled *Reader's Digest*, which was extremely popular in the United States.[116] A week later, Schiffrin, who was surprised to say the least, replied, "But have you ever actually seen a *Reader's Digest*? I'm sending you a copy. You can decide for yourself how similar it is to your book!"[117]

Schiffrin had also been called upon to facilitate or participate in various projects during the war. Robert Aron, a former colleague of Schiffrin's from his time at Gallimard, wrote to him from Algiers, after fleeing France because he was Jewish. He wrote to Schiffrin in 1943 to ask him to participate in a new literary review. The journal was called *L'Arche* and had been founded in Algiers with the help of André Gide and one of his friends, a young poet from the Kabyle region of Algeria named Jean Amrouche. *L'Arche* had the goal of temporarily replacing the *NRF*, which was then under the editorship of the fascist collaborator Drieu la Rochelle, as the leading French literary journal. As Robert Aron wrote on October 8, 1943, "We want to create a French literary review, perhaps a new kind, but in any case, one that is dignified and free, not too Drieu la Rochelle."[118] Aron hoped that with Schiffrin's help, other important figures in exile in the United States would also contribute to the project. In particular, Aron named Denis de Rougemont, Julien Green, Jacques Maritain, and André Breton, writers who were in contact with Schiffrin during the war. Aron hoped that Schiffrin would act as his "United States correspondent," with the mission of distributing the review in the United States, as well as sending texts to

Algiers by authors with whom he was in contact. In December 1943, when the first issue of the review was published, Aron wrote to Schiffrin, insisting that he "consider himself the editor-in-chief of the American edition."[119] While Robert Aron was presenting himself as the director of the review, Gide wrote to Schiffrin on February 13, 1944, to explain the true situation. The *L'Arche* project, the first issue of which was published in February 1944, was important, of course, but Aron was far from heading it. Gide wrote,

> I would be very grateful if you could find us some customers for the good, well-written works in French published in *L'Arche*, and help make the review that is so dear to my heart a success. I know that in his letters, Robert Aron has a tendency to appear as its director: This is not the truth . . . quite the contrary. I was asked to come back to Algiers to get everything in good order.[120]

In fact, while he was asking Schiffrin for articles for *L'Arche*, Aron was steering another ship: *La Nef*, a monthly review first published in July 1944, which he directed after splitting from *L'Arche*. Despite these petty rivalries, which tended to dishearten him, Schiffrin remained the person everyone solicited to act as a correspondent in New York, since he was considered an excellent facilitator of the various elements of the French literary community during World War II spread among New York, North Africa, and France.

Even though Schiffrin was in contact with the other side of the Atlantic to create international literary reviews, it was in New York that most new projects were being born, including those created by Europeans in exile: The Surrealists, led by André Breton, launched *VVV*, while the *École libre des Hautes Études* started its own publication called *Renaissance*.[121]

Beyond the important figures in French literature also living in New York, like Breton, Soupault, Maurois, Green, Maritain and Saint-Exupéry, Schiffrin was also in touch with the world of Russian-speaking exiles, including Souvarine, Alexeïeff, and Rachel Bespaloff, the author of *De l'Iliade* (*On the Iliad*), published by Pantheon. Schiffrin's literary and intellectual correspondence with Rachel Bespaloff is illustrated in a letter from 1944:

> One thing strikes me. Fragonard and Péguy were haunted by *Antigone*. Our age is obsessed by *Electra*. It is truly the time of *Electra*. Take Sartre's *No Exit* for example: Hell is the absence of charity. Take Camus' *The Misunderstanding*: Hell (for the mother also speaks of Hell at the end), Hell is the absence of charity— and it is also the absence of liberty.[122]

Schiffrin wanted Hermann Broch, an Austrian Jew in exile in New York during the war, to write the preface for *De l'Iliade*. When he could not get in touch with Broch, Hannah Arendt, who had also taken refuge in the United States during the war, let Schiffrin know how Broch's work on *The Sleepwalkers* was going.[123]

André Schiffrin recounts the atmosphere in New York at this time and his father's friendship with Arendt:

> I remember my father's evenings of discussions with [Meyer] Schapiro,[124] Hannah Arendt, and others. The French, German and Austrian exiles, such as the novelist Hermann Broch, felt very close. With Arendt, in part due to years of her Paris exile, my parents shared not only a common past, but the travails of their American existence. It would be many years before Arendt would find even the most modest of teaching posts; before that,

she worked at part-time jobs with Jewish organizations and later
for the German-exile publisher Schocken. Meanwhile, she could
identify with my father, who had been close to several German
publishers during the Weimar years. . . . I was allowed to sit in on
these evenings of talk, and it made me think that my parents were
part of a vital and important intellectual world.[125]

Meyer Schapiro was born in what is today Lithuania, Hannah
Arendt in Hanover, Hermann Broch in Vienna, and Jacques
Schiffrin in Baku, but it was New York, in the context of World
War II and exile, that brought them together. Hannah Arendt
was the private tutor of André and Simone Schiffrin for a while;
she "taught us as if she was at Harvard, with passion and preci-
sion and without the slightest hint of embarrassment or conde-
scension,"[126] as Jacques's son recalls in his autobiography.

Schiffrin was also a member of several associations, such
as the Gaullist organization France Forever, which shaped
his editorial choices both at Jacques Schiffrin & Co. and at
Pantheon Books. From New York, and in his own way, Jacques
Schiffrin wanted to be a Resistance publisher, and the writers
and books he published reflected this. Faithful to his literary
passion, he was a devoted member of the Balzac Society of
America.[127]

In many ways, life in New York City was good for Jacques
Schiffrin. He was publishing and in conversation with some of
the most brilliant minds of the time. He sold books throughout the Americas and corresponded with the most important
French literary and political figures. Despite all this, the tor-
ment he felt in the early days of his arrival in America, escaping
from the looming danger in Europe, continued to haunt him.
His constant activity, his meetings, and his ongoing correspondence with friends and colleagues served as a way to keep his

mind occupied. And, of course, with Pantheon Books, Jacques Schiffrin had rediscovered the joys of publishing, a career he loved that gave meaning to his life. But what about his personal life? In April 1944, when Jacques Schiffrin's life was no longer as difficult as when he had first arrived in New York, he wrote to André Gide, "Here I am, getting older. I've been so battered (as you've seen . . .) that I can't manage to recover and feel I am only half alive."[128]

Feeling "half alive" would take on a new dimension for Schiffrin once the war ended. Oddly enough, by the time Paris was liberated in August 1944, Jacques Schiffrin was beginning to establish himself in the New York publishing world, after three years of trial and error. Once Paris had been liberated and France became France again, why not go back, given that he had never felt totally at home in New York and had not fully recovered from the pain of exile?

3

THE IMPOSSIBLE RETURN

B y 1944, the winds of freedom had drifted from America, where Jacques Schiffrin now lived, to Normandy, where he had joined Gaston Gallimard at the beginning of World War II. Soon Paris, then Europe, would be liberated. In the Schiffrins' living room, an enormous map, taken from the *New York Times*, allowed the family to follow the events of the conflict.[1] Once the war was over, many of the French immigrants in New York chose to return to Europe. Jacques Schiffrin wanted to go back. He felt nostalgic, a feeling that had haunted him since his arrival in New York and would never quite leave him. Having started in America with nothing, he had built a new life and a powerful publishing business in New York. And yet Europe was still in his thoughts.

Schiffrin wanted to go back but couldn't. His health as much as his professional considerations would not allow it. Times had changed. Although Gallimard had written to Schiffrin repeatedly as soon as the war ended, Schiffrin understood only too well that he belonged to "the world of yesterday" and that as a man over fifty, it would be difficult for him to start over again. So it was his son, André, who was sent across the Atlantic in 1949 to see his father's friends—Gide, whose first name he shared, and

Roger Martin du Gard, as well as the "*NRF* madmen," including Gaston Gallimard, whom he had liked teasing when he was a child in France. Jacques Schiffrin was passing the baton on to his only son and to a new generation. If he was to remain in exile in New York, André would be given the knowledge and experience that would allow him to live on both sides of the Atlantic.

NOSTALGIA

When the war ended, everyone who had been in exile in New York was talking about going back to Europe. Jacques Schiffrin was homesick. This is obvious in his letters and was confirmed by his family and friends. This feeling of homesickness was compounded by his awareness of the extreme difficulty—if not impossibility—of realizing his dream.

At the same time, Schiffrin's nostalgia intensified with the absence of prospects: Even if he could return to France with no concern over his safety, he would be anxious about what awaited him on his return.

Paris continued to haunt Jacques Schiffrin, yet the French capital had not completely forgotten the former director of the *Pléiade*. During the war, in April 1942, Maria van Rysselberghe, Gide's faithful friend, wrote in her *Notebooks*, "[Gide] is giving me a copy of his *Journal*, knowing that the copy he wanted me to have had been left in Schiffrin's office."[2] Jacques Schiffrin's friends wanted to believe that he still had an office in Paris. But along with that now nonexistent office, he had left his books, his furniture, and many memories.

Those in exile in New York during the war formed many plans to try to return home based on strategies that depended primarily on their country of origin. For the French community in exile, returning was a definite option. For most French men and women who had taken refuge in New York, the collapse of the Vichy government and the defeat of the Nazis throughout Europe signaled the end of the catastrophic years during which France had been robbed of its freedom. As most had opposed the Vichy regime, they could seriously and confidently envisage going home. For the Germans in exile, however, the situation was very different: It was almost impossible to imagine returning to a country that had so brutally caused such horror. To the French, however, their country would once more become the eternal France as incarnated by de Gaulle and betrayed by Vichy. For the Germans in exile, many of whom were Jewish, the same was not possible: They had lost all hope and no longer believed in their country. Albert Einstein died in Princeton in 1955, and Kurt Wolff, who continued running Pantheon Books after the war, died in New York in 1963, having never returned to Germany.

As we have seen, Jacques Schiffrin's unusual journey allowed him to mix in several different circles, putting him in contact with as many Russian and German individuals in exile as French. Because he worked for a publishing house that was global in reach and cosmopolitan in attitude, he was more open-minded than many French refugees in New York, who mostly kept to themselves. Moreover, Schiffrin had learned English, which many French exiles had not troubled to do. Jacques Schiffrin's Jewishness was also an element when considering returning to France. Emmanuelle Loyer describes how certain Jews were anxious about returning:

> The uncertainty concerning the eradication of a type of anti-Semitism that some certainly did not consider completely non-native led to hesitation over the decision to return. . . . There was a line separating French Jews from those who had recently been

naturalized during the war or had remained foreigners, and they were more skeptical about the welcome they might receive.[3]

(Jacques Schiffrin had become a naturalized French citizen in 1927.) To some, the conflict between the desire to return to a past that had been lost and the necessity of remaining in a present that could never resemble that past led to extreme actions. Many committed suicide, including Stefan Zweig in Brazil in 1942 and Jacques Schiffrin's friend, the writer Rachel Bespaloff, who took her life in the United States in April 1949.

Schiffrin's deep desire to return home and continual concern regarding life "over there" is prominent throughout his correspondence. Letters became a way of maintaining a link between the "here" of New York and the "there" of Paris. The exchanges between André Gide and Jacques Schiffrin are full of allusions to a possible return. On January 4, 1944, Schiffrin confided to Gide, "Especially am thinking about over there. When will I see you again? Come over to America!! Or will we perhaps soon be coming to you?"[4] And in April of the same year, Schiffrin once again persisted: "When, my God, will we see each other again? It's been so long!"[5]

Jacques Schiffrin seemed to be constantly thinking about the French capital, his thoughts and mood dependent on the fate of the city during the war. As he wrote on June 5, 1944, "Today Rome was taken. We're thinking of Paris."[6] Though he had little choice, Jacques Schiffrin had left friends, family members, and so many others he was concerned about and toward whom he simultaneously felt a form of guilt: the guilt of having escaped. Thus, in July 1944, Schiffrin wrote to Gide once again:

We never forget how shamefully privileged we are and barely dare to think about the people we will see again (or won't see again . . .): Simone's family, mine, our friends. . . . Have you any news of what's happening in France? What about Catherine, Mme Théo, Roger Martin du Gard, and the rest? Tell me.[7]

At the beginning of January 1945, the situation remained the same: constant anxiety over those who had remained in Europe and plans to return that Schiffrin passionately wished for but were continually thwarted. At the same time, he was reminded of the terrible suffering he went through when he left France, which he did not wish to relive:

> What horrible news . . . from over there. Deaths, deportations. . . . How many friends we will never see again? I had a telegram from Boris de Schloezer. I was so relieved! When I left him he was very ill. I was constantly worried about him. We're thinking about coming back. Not right away: There are still many formalities, still no ships, etc. All this is so painful.[8]

Moreover, Jacques Schiffrin's health seriously compromised any plans to return; the emphysema he contracted at the beginning of the war was still intruding on his daily life, causing him to grow weaker. In July 1945, he complained about his health, as if fate, once more, were conspiring against him:

> When, oh my God! When will I see you all again? My return will be delayed, alas! My doctor is seriously opposed to it. My state of health is not brilliant: I've lost more weight (I'm down to 108 pounds). I have to gain some weight. And my emphysema forces me to take every precaution possible, which would be difficult to do, for now, from the other side of the ocean. So I have no choice but to resign myself to wait.[9]

Less than 110 pounds at nearly five feet, eleven inches, Jacques Schiffrin was weak and exhausted. Nevertheless, he suggested a possible trip to France at the beginning of August 1945: "Yes, I'm looking after myself and doing what I can, so I can return."[10] In October, his desire to see Paris again seemed stronger than ever: "We think of nothing but returning!"[11] But his condition left him no choice: Schiffrin was forced to remain in New York. In a letter dated March 1946 to his old friend Jef Last, with whom he had accompanied Gide to the USSR, Schiffrin expressed his angst: "What can I tell you about me? I've aged a hundred years. Always disgusted! And with good reason, you have to admit."[12]

As Pierre Paul Royer-Collard (1763–1845), a member of the French Academy, once said, "At my age, one no longer reads, one re-reads." Schiffrin had thus begun to re-read the classics and the works of his close friends. At the end of the summer of 1946, he started re-reading *La Porte étroite* (*Strait is the Gate*) by his faithful friend André Gide.[13] The editor also immersed himself in books he had read in his youth, as he explained to Roger Martin du Gard in April 1948: "To do something different, I recently re-read *War and Peace*, to rediscover all the friends we love so much."[14] In 1949, he re-read the nostalgic novel par excellence and wrote to Gide, "I've just re-read [Proust's] *Le Temps retrouvé* [*Time Regained*]. . . . If I wait any longer, I won't recognize anyone."[15] He also listened to classical music on the radio, including works by Chopin and Mozart, pieces that brought back memories of Europe and his early years in Paris, as he explained in a letter written in May 1947:

> Music is a wonderful—and the only—comfort I have here, thanks to the radio and the profusion of magnificent concerts. Apart from that—nothing, nothing. And especially no friends. It's my

friends I miss most terribly, and you are over there. I'm toying with the idea of coming to see you next spring.[16]

In New York, Schiffrin had many acquaintances but few real friends. As Schiffrin wrote to Gide in October 1949, "Music is a great comfort here. And reading. But 'the flesh is sad, alas! . . .'[17] All I do is re-read books, your *Journal* among others."[18] Jacques Schiffrin's nostalgia was not only affected by space, but also by time. He longed for Paris, where he had true friends and where his melancholy constantly led him. All that remained for him was an impossible dream: to live out his days in the sun of the Midi, to forget the infinite sadness of his years in exile:

> Just think: it is six years to the day that we left. Six years that have gone by ridiculously quickly. The most bleak, empty years of my life. . . . I have the impression that here, life is unraveling and dwindling. . . . I would like to live out the rest of my days in France, in the Midi. I must "find a way to."[19]

In the letters he exchanged with Roger Martin du Gard, his nostalgia was even more intense. Throughout their long correspondence, Martin du Gard tried to comfort his friend, encouraging him to fight his nostalgia by pointing out the advantages of his departure for the United States. But Martin du Gard's insistence undoubtedly reflected how much Schiffrin missed Europe, so he tried to console his friend:

> But don't complain too much, dear friend; no matter how painful your exile might be, no matter how difficult your life might be, regret nothing. . . . Just think of how many people envy you for being over there and who wouldn't hesitate to exchange their life

on the run for the burden you feel as an exile and your material concerns! No, no, regret nothing, you are not the worst off. . . . You mustn't compare the life you once had with your current life, rather with the circumstances you would have had to face here. If you are truly aware of that, you will easily fight the temptation to feel regret![20]

To Martin du Gard, Schiffrin must not, and should not, complain: Compared with the difficulty of life in France, the man in exile had no legitimate reason to bemoan his fate. In May 1945, at the end of the war, Martin du Gard reiterated this message:

What are your plans? Are you staying there for good? I imagine that in spite of everything, you still feel nostalgia for Europe and your past? . . . Don't rush to give in to it! Europe and the past are nothing more than rubble; and there remains so much general distress that even the most spectacular of the "Victories" would be unable to make us feel optimistic again.[21]

Even though Martin du Gard warned Schiffrin not to give in to his nostalgia, Schiffrin still wished to see his friend again. On January 17, 1947, Martin du Gard validated this desire while continuing to scorn the publisher's nostalgia: "I don't want to criticize your nostalgia, since it will no doubt lead you to come back to us. (Once you get here, you will immediately feel nostalgia for back there!)"[22]

By December 1947, Jacques Schiffrin's illness had taken a turn for the worse, and his hopes of seeing his "sweet France" again were fading. In April 1948, he wrote to Roger Martin du Gard a letter full of sadness over the fact that his emphysema would prevent him from carrying out his plan to return:

I think of you every day—and that is not a metaphor; I wonder
(but don't say that I'm "Russian" or anything like that! . . .) if you
haven't completely forgotten me? What I wouldn't give to see you
again, good God! But that would take the mountain (you) coming
to the prophet. For, alas! My journey to sweet France is becoming
more problematic every day. I wrote to you (a century ago!) that
I suffered from a nasty type of emphysema, that it was getting
harder and harder for me to breathe. I was wrong to complain:
I lived a more or less normal life, going to the office every day,
going out occasionally in the evening, etc. . . . And then, one day
at the end of last December, for no reason whatsoever, I was completely unable to breathe and felt exhausted, without the strength
to even move. I've been at home for four months now, in bed half
of the time. Three weeks in the hospital, in an oxygen tent, did
nothing. I drag myself around like a dying man, with no strength
and unable to breathe.[23]

Sadness for the loss of his homeland was also fed by a
kind of pessimism, an absence of hope that was understandable during the war but which became more problematic after
France had been liberated. In 1947, Jacques Schiffrin wrote to
Jean Paulhan, who had replaced him as director of the *Pléiade*.
He explained he was feeling nostalgic while re-reading some
old letters Paulhan had sent him before the war, letters he had
just received:

A few days ago, I received a small box from Paris containing a
few books and letters I particularly wanted and which, at the last
moment before leaving Paris (in '40), I was able to safely hide
(the rest of my library—nine-tenths—as well as everything we
had in our apartment, was taken by the Germans immediately
after we left).[24]

To understand Schiffrin's feelings, it is necessary to remember that he and his family left France surrounded by violence and in fear for their lives. He seemed unable to return, not only because of his illness, but also because he could *not* return, because it was impossible for him to forget the circumstances that forced him into exile. In a letter dated January 13, 1947, to Jean Paulhan, Schiffrin insisted on this point. Six years after he had left, after he had broken with France, the wound had not healed:

> Do you know the story of the men from Marseille who are bragging, talking about their exploits during the war? One of them, however, says nothing: "Well what about you, Marius? Don't you have a story to tell?" "I have nothing to say because I was killed at Verdun." As for me, my dear Paulhan, I was killed at Montoire, more precisely by Hitler. . . . I cannot manage to "forget"—and all the anger I felt is still within me. But to talk about that would make me cross a line.[25]

At Montoire, on October 24, 1940, Marshal Pétain met Hitler. On November 5, 1940, Gaston Gallimard dismissed Jacques Schiffrin. On May 20, 1941, Schiffrin left France via Marseille. He simply could not manage to forget his dismissal. And the final words of this letter to Paulhan reveal how much Jacques Schiffrin was still suffering at the end of the war.

Unlike many French refugees in New York, Schiffrin truly had no choice: His departure was literally a matter of life or death. Where returning was concerned, his situation was perhaps closer to that of the German exiles for whom Germany could never again be the Germany of Goethe. "Killed in Montoire, more precisely by Hitler," Schiffrin, even after the war, could not forget. In some way, Jacques Schiffrin felt nostalgia for his own life, the one he had lost.

A PUBLISHER FROM THE WORLD
OF YESTERDAY[26]

Jacques Schiffrin wanted to return but could not. Both his illness and his memories prevented it, but he also had doubts about his ability to reestablish himself in a France that would never be quite the same.

In 1944, after the liberation of France, Gallimard got in touch. The *Pléiade* had continued to exist throughout the war. Gaston Gallimard had even continued to try to make it a showcase of his publishing house by organizing so-called "*Pléiade* concerts," which allowed literary Paris to gather to enjoy classical music. In 1943, a Pléiade Prize was established to be awarded to a promising young author. Among the panel of judges were Jean Paulhan, Albert Camus, Maurice Blanchot, Paul Éluard, and André Malraux.[27]

If Drieu la Rochelle's *Nouvelle Revue Française* was considered the dirty branch of Gallimard's publishing enterprise during the war, the *Pléiade* remained the credible branch, almost an enclave of resistance, or at least proof of respectability. Between 1940 and 1945, under Jean Paulhan's direction, the *Pléiade* published just ten works, compared with forty-three between 1933 and 1939.[28] During the war, Schiffrin's ghost and standards of excellence continued to haunt the collection. Among the books published during this period, many were thanks to Jacques Schiffrin, who had overseen part of their production before fleeing France. As the end of hostilities approached, the question of his return was openly discussed at Gallimard. On April 21, 1944, Paulhan, who was still in charge of the prestigious collection, took the initiative and wrote to his friend: "We're all still alive, and that's already a very good thing. It would be good to meet soon (and to talk of something other than the war.) So when are you going to come and reclaim your *Pléiade*?"[29] As early as

June 1942, André Gide had already spoken up: "It remains, and will remain, whatever might or could happen, that the *Pléiade* is your masterpiece. Everyone says so and knows it; and will know it."[30]

September 11, 1944. After many long years of embarrassed silence, the Gallimards made contact. It was not Gaston, who had written the letter of November 5, 1940, dismissing Jacques Schiffrin, but his brother Raymond who wrote:

My dear friend,

After four years I can finally write to you, and that makes me very happy. I've just had your news from your brother and I hope to very soon have news of you yourself, while waiting for you to come back to us. I'm eager to have details about you and your family. . . .

We have done everything possible to keep the *Pléiade* going as best we could during your absence, and I hope that you won't find it in too bad a state when you return. The next books to be published are the *Complete Works of Mallarmé* and *War and Peace*; a collection by Rimbaud is in preparation.

But what I especially wish to tell you is how much I have thought of you while you were so far away from us, and how impatiently I look forward to your return.

Do not worry at all about your financial situation when you arrive. Your account was put in order when you left; since then, we have given 167,000 francs to your in-laws, and there is another 300,000 francs still in your account. But if that is not sufficient, I am—please know this—at your disposal.

I would be delighted to see you as soon as possible, and I hope that you will tell me when you will be coming very soon.

Warmest wishes,
Raymond Gallimard[31]

What was Schiffrin's reaction to such a letter? Joy at knowing he hadn't been forgotten? That his position might be waiting for him on the other side of the Atlantic? Or anger, fury, and cynicism in the face of words that attempted to erase four years of pain that the Gallimard brothers could not even begin to imagine? Whatever the case may be, it is clear that at the end of the war, the most important people at Gallimard—Jean Paulhan and Raymond Gallimard—imagined Schiffrin's return as a matter of course.

Jacques also received other letters signed by Gaston, as he explained to André Gide on December 2, 1944:

> I had some letters from Gaston and Raymond: My brother (the filmmaker) who is in charge of the Cinematic Services of the French government, saw the two Gallimard brothers in Paris (it was he—my brother—who brought me these letters from Paris where he had gone for work). Gaston wrote to me, saying that "what he holds dearest to his heart is to see me return." Raymond told me the same thing, but in a tone that sounded much more sincere. . . . Do you have news of the publishing house?[32]

A few weeks later, Gide confirmed Gaston Gallimard's desire to have Jacques Schiffrin return, but the question of his resuming his role as director of the *Pléiade* remained unresolved:

> I finally received a letter from Gaston Gallimard—who told me he truly wishes you to return to Paris, and that "he had a large amount of money at his disposal." There's just the question of whether you would take up the position of director of the *Pléiade* again. . . . (This question comes from me).[33]

In 1945, Raymond Gallimard continued writing to Jacques Schiffrin, expressing impatience for his return. "Your brother tells me that you hope to come back soon; I'm greatly looking forward to that moment. . . . We could then get back into our old routine," he wrote on April 16.[34] And in the same vein on November 17:

> But when do you think you'll come back? I would be very happy to see you again and I'm still waiting to hear that you've arrived. The *Pléiade* is also waiting for you to return; for the moment, Paulhan is in charge of it, along with me; the more we think about the collection, the more new titles we find to publish.[35]

But as time passed, Jacques Schiffrin's return seemed in ever greater jeopardy. Although Gallimard proved unwilling or hesitant to take Schiffrin back, the French publishing house worked with Schiffrin on some projects in the United States. In October 1945, Schiffrin suggested that the Gallimard brothers participate in the publication of the *Anthologie de la poésie française* (*Anthology of French Poetry*), edited by Gide for the *Pléiade*. Schiffrin also asked the Gallimards if they would agree to cede the rights for an American publication in French, presumably for publication in the French Pantheon Books collection.[36] Raymond was quick to respond: "I must admit quite openly that we are against publishing French works by American publishers," mainly in the name of "a policy of defending French publishing."[37] This, however, did not prevent Gaston and Raymond from claiming they sincerely hoped that Schiffrin would return: "We truly wish you were here in Paris (and "we" includes all the Gallimards)," as Gide wrote to his friend in November.[38] With no bitterness, Schiffrin sent cigars to Raymond Gallimard from New York through his brother Simon.[39] In return, Schiffrin received "a complete *Pléiade* collection."[40] In spite of the rejections and mistrust, Jacques Schiffrin and Gallimard would never completely sever their ties.

In May 1946, Raymond Gallimard traveled to New York and met with Jacques Schiffrin.[41] Perhaps they discussed the project Schiffrin had described to André Gide in September 1946:

A new publishing house is being set up that will publish, in French and English, the entire *NRF* collection (have the Gallimards talked to you about this?). Without leaving Pantheon, where I am in charge of the entire publishing process, the publications of the new publishing house will operate under my "American eye." And I very much want us to "open fire" with your works. We will no longer allow American publishers to behave like the dog in the Russian proverb who, "lying in the hay, doesn't eat it and doesn't let anyone else eat it." They (the American publishers) will have to either republish—or bring out previously unpublished—works, and if they don't, we will do it. I have several projects in mind and will talk to you about them very soon.[42]

Jacques Schiffrin found himself in the same position as that of the South American publishers who wanted to distribute works he had published in New York. Except this time, the entire *NRF* catalog was involved, as well as the creation of a publishing house specifically designed to distribute its works in the United States. Gide's enthusiasm for this project was understandable: "I am very excited by the projects you've discussed with me: a publishing house that would take the entire *NRF* collection and republish it in America, with you as its director. Bravo! I applaud this with all my heart."[43] But time passed, and nothing happened: The project was to remain a dream.

Schiffrin was also involved with *Les Cahiers de la Pléiade* (*The Pléiade Notebooks*), which briefly replaced the *Nouvelle Revue Française* owing to the fallout from the journal's collaboration with the Nazis and the Vichy regime. *Les Cahiers de la Pléiade* was a literary review published by Gallimard and edited by Jean Paulhan, who had succeeded Schiffrin as director of the *Pléiade* in 1940. The review was published thirteen times between 1946 and 1952, until the *NRF* resumed publication in 1953. During its publication run, *Les Cahiers de la Pléiade* published works by "classic" writers such as Gide but also new authors who Paulhan wanted to promote, including Maurice Blanchot and Francis Ponge.

However, in reviewing it for Paulhan, Schiffrin pulled no punches:

> You've also asked me for my "critique" on Issue n°1 of the *Cahiers de la Pléiade* (we're talking about copy edits, of course, but let me tell you how much I liked your *Petit Guide*).
>
> Well! I don't really like the font very much ("Europe"): Its only virtue is that it is "modern." (But I think it's the kind of "modern" that becomes dated very quickly.) I think that for the publicity texts—and especially because there aren't many all at once, this font works quite well with novelty fonts. In itself, it lacks charm; it's a bit dull and monotonous. I also don't really care for your opting for a large margin at the top of the page and almost none at the bottom (a big head with legs that are too short). Finally, the vertical line on each page makes me think of an accounting ledger. . . . The cover is very pretty. I have the impression that he was trying to be "unusual" as they say in English. Was it Picasso who said, "People who seek don't interest me. Only those who find"? . . .
>
> I hope you won't find my criticism too "cutting" or "excessive" (that would upset me greatly.)[44]

In a letter to André Gide in 1949, Schiffrin added more:

> It seems to me that without the *Pléiade*, Gallimard would seriously need an "artistic eye," for what they are doing is horrible. The Proust illustrated by van Dongen is an outrage. Your illustrated

"works of the imagination" is as well. Where the hell! did they find the abominable decorations on the title pages (the worst is 1900), those hideous end pieces? Is it Festy or Raymond? Is it possible that it came from Roger Allard? Never mind. I have my own taste when it comes to typography and I'm sharing it with them. (By the way: Did you receive our edition of Saint-John Perse's *Exile*, which I found very well done?)[45]

Jacques Schiffrin's acerbic view of the editorial and aesthetic judgment of the works produced by Gallimard revealed both his professional view and, undoubtedly, a kind of personal resentment toward the publishing house that had caused him so many problems. Despite this, Schiffrin continued to hope that he would someday return to Gallimard. In June 1949, he got in touch with Raymond Gallimard, as he explained to André Gide:

> Just think: After eight years here, I'm only earning half of what it would take to live simply. And not one friend, almost no acquaintances (*bekannte*); it's like a jungle. And so!! I wrote to Raymond to ask him if he would take me back at the *NRF—Pléiade*. His reply: "Since unable to offer me a position that I deserve (sic!), he prefers not to offer anything." In the meantime, the *Pléiade* made them, and continues to make them, millions—and me, not a bean! The blows keep coming! So that is that.[46]

But reality intervened. Schiffrin was then fifty-seven, and a new generation had taken over Gallimard in Paris. This is what Gide tried to make his friend understand in July 1949, while consoling him and reminding him that the great *Pléiade* collection remained his legacy:

> As for the *Pléiade* business, my heart is heavy, and I intend to speak at length about it with Gaston or Raymond Gallimard. . . .

The extraordinary success of the *Pléiade* IS DUE TO YOU; they seem to be forgetting that far too much. I want to discuss with the Gallimard brothers whether there might be a way to offer you the possibility of taking over complete control of the collection. That would be, in my opinion, the only honest, honorable way—for them and for you—to come back to work for the publishing house. . . . But Raymond's evasive reply, which you've sent me, hasn't made me indignant. He must have been terribly embarrassed; anyone would be, and for even less. What could he say?? Many pages wouldn't be enough to explain that to you. . . . What position might you want that isn't already taken? How could X or Y hand over his job? And what job would we be talking about? It would be beneath you to accept a junior position.[47]

Roger Martin du Gard was also well aware of the problem, explaining to André Gide in June 1949,

The least unreasonable solution would be to find a place for him [Schiffrin] at the *NRF*. . . . There he could use his many skills. (But they don't want to have him back. And he would find an *NRF* littered with new factions that risk being hostile to him, people who would slowly, pitilessly reject him.)[48]

Writing to Schiffrin at the beginning of July 1949, Martin du Gard was unequivocal:

Let's not even discuss the *NRF*. It's lucky for you they don't even believe they are obliged to offer you a job. You would have accepted, and it would have been a catastrophe. The atmosphere there is not like it used to be. The young ones, the newcomers, have enormous influence. You would have been eliminated once and for all, subject to silent hostility you would have found intolerable.

Even the vocabulary has changed. You would feel more like a foreigner than you do in America![49]

There was a "before the war," and an "after the war." There was an "Old Guard" and a "New Guard." Schiffrin was born in the nineteenth century, and his great friends were André Gide and Roger Martin du Gard, but Jean-Paul Sartre and Albert Camus now dominated the world of letters.

In a long letter to Jacques Schiffrin on January 17, 1947, Roger Martin du Gard describes himself as a man of the former world, overtaken by events. And he considers the former director of *Pléiade* his alter ego, his anachronistic companion:

> Our misfortune, for both of us, was to be born in this period of chaos and stabbing insecurity, with temperaments and sensitivities that are particularly badly equipped to adapt to such instability. But we are stuck with what we have been given. . . . We feel like we have been in a shipwreck, where everything we hold dear is about to sink. Perhaps this is just an illusion? Perhaps we simply find ourselves caught up in one of those enormous historical upheavals that means epochs of profound mutation to humanity and are the very conditions necessary for man's progress? We think we are at the bottom of an abyss. But these convulsions that affect the world, that make us see things upside down, perhaps they are the contractions that accompany childbirth? Perhaps our descendants will regard the current period in history as a glorious moment of regeneration, the beginning of the "new era" they will be proud to be the first to lead.

This analysis placed Schiffrin and Martin du Gard among the last survivors of yesterday's world, with World War II as the fundamental break with the past.

Martin du Gard took no pleasure in the new Paris that had taken on the frenetic activity of modernity:

> We are not young enough or have enough nerve to bear this exis-
> tence under the whip, this daily "do or die," which is the rhythm
> of all the capitals of this world of madmen. I feel myself devoid of
> substance in this life, dispossessed of myself. However, the people
> you see here are not living *their* life, but a collective life, in which
> everyone thinks and speaks only in the headlines of the week; they
> change every Sunday, after reading the weekly newspapers. . . .
> Wherever you go, in the corridors of the *NRF*, in the intermis-
> sions of new plays, at performances, everyone has the same con-
> cerns, says the same things, repeats the same petty lies, slips the
> same jokes into conversations all week long.[50]

Why would Jacques Schiffrin want to return to such a world? Gide was ill, exhausted, and rarely went out. Martin du Gard could no longer stand the pace of the times.

One is reminded of the final meeting between Deslauriers and Frédéric Moreau in the final chapter of *Sentimental Education*: "Then they blamed chance, circumstances, the age into which they had been born." Flaubert meant to be ironic, but, for the likes of Schiffrin, Gide, and Martin du Gard, the great names of the Old World did not really have a place in the France of the thirty-year postwar boom—or even in post–World War II Europe. For those who had built their lives and careers before the war, it was difficult, if not impossible, to hold a prominent place after the war.

In January 1945, Jean-Paul Sartre, who represented the new cultural and intellectual mood of Paris, visited New York. Sent by the newspapers *Combat* and *Le Figaro*, he made a point of meeting with Jacques and Simone Schiffrin. They had an enjoyable dinner during which everyone drank, laughed, and got along well. To a certain extent, Sartre had come to visit an important person in the New World, the Schiffrin who had made a career in New York, the city of the future. But in truth, Jacques Schiffrin was already an incarnation of the past. The *Pléiade* represented the "Old Guard," and Schiffrin was associated with his Nobel Prize–winning friends, whom Sartre only reluctantly admired.[51] Sartre, like many of his contemporaries, was immersed in existentialism and Heidegger. He had been thinking and writing during the war and had already published *L'Être et le néant* (*Being and Nothingness*). Unlike Schiffrin, he had not been forced to merely survive. When questioned about the exiles in New York who feared being scorned if they

FIGURE 3.1 Jacques Schiffrin, Simone Schiffrin, and Jean-Paul Sartre in New York, January 1945. (Schiffrin family personal archives.)

returned home, Sartre gave this chilling reply: "It's much worse; they've been forgotten."[52]

What Sartre said may have been harsh, but it nevertheless embodied the reality faced by certain exiles. As time passed, the irremediable distance that increased between the men of yesterday and the men of the postwar era became a major cause of Jacques Schiffrin's reluctance to return to France. Among the "Old Guard," Schiffrin had not been forgotten. Martin du Gard and Gide continued writing to him, but to all the new "*NRF* madmen*," and to all the young writers who had begun publishing after the war, Jacques Schiffrin was someone who was well and truly gone, both in time and space: He belonged to a different world.

Jacques Schiffrin may have belonged to yesterday's world, but he was also the father of a young boy who was ten years old in 1945, the incarnation of hope for the future. In 1948, Roger Martin du Gard asked for news of André:

> You haven't given me any news about your young American son. What kind of things does he like; what does he want to be? And what does he think of old, decrepit, bitter Europe? The young European generation is destined for more unhappiness than joy. You are living in a country where personal happiness is still more or less possible, for those who have adapted to the place. That will be your consolation, and something that will compensate for your nostalgia as an exile.[53]

The future was there, and his name was André. And as compensation for his nostalgia as an exile, to accomplish what he himself was no longer capable of doing, it was his son, André, whom Jacques would send across the Atlantic. André Schiffrin was about to begin his "political education."

ANDRÉ'S JOURNEY

When André was fourteen years old, Jacques Schiffrin sent him to Europe. In his autobiography, André Schiffrin explains the reasons his parents encouraged him to undertake the crossing:

> So my parents had different motives for sending me back, none of which I realized. They wanted me to rediscover France, but at the same time I was something of an advance guard, feeling out the territory to see what it would be like there for all of us. Later I realized that I had been like the dove sent from Noah's ark to see what life was left after the flood.[54]

Too exhausted, both physically and emotionally, to go himself, Jacques Schiffrin chose to have his son carry out the journey he had dreamed of. By doing so, he also allowed his son to fully understand his own personal history, the world from which he came. In this maiden voyage, André was to be both his father's representative, visiting his old friends and former colleagues, and a sign of hope, a "dove" as André Schiffrin put it, observing the Old World with the frankness of youth.

What was André's life like in New York before this trip? Quite soon after the Schiffrins arrived in New York, André was sent to a boarding school in Montclair, New Jersey, founded mainly for the children of French refugees. The school was called *La Petite Maison de France* (The Little French House) and was run by a woman named Jeanne Blanc.[55] When his parents told him they wanted to send him to boarding school, André was fiercely opposed to the idea:

> I was appalled by this prospect of separation and argued strongly against it, saying that I could be a happy latchkey child and wait if

need be on the doorstep. The last thing I wanted to do was move again; fear of being uprooted was the one trauma that I clearly felt.[56]

His parents had the last word, however, and André spent weekdays in Montclair, coming home on weekends to explore New York and its surroundings with his parents. At boarding school, André drew a lot: More than mere doodles, he drew pictures of his "Paradise Lost," the France he had to leave at the age of five. The young Minouche drew the "Toure Eiffel"—misspelling it—under a large sun, as seen from the "Champ de Mars." There was also the "Arc de Triomphe in the Middle of the Place de l'Étoile," also under a beautiful sun, with a plane flying past. And then there was his "Place de la Concorde," which he described as "the most beautiful square in the world." At the bottom of this drawing, enormous boats the size of the Luxor Obelisk float along the Seine. These drawings demonstrated the extent to which France filled the young boy's imagination, and from a very early age. In one drawing of "Biarritz, a Grand, Chic Beach on the Mediterranean," we find the same large boats present in his drawing of the Seine sailing along the Atlantic coast, as André Schiffrin imagined them. At the bottom of a letter André wrote to his parents on August 21, 1942, in which he talks about his daily routine, he drew three large ships with the French flag flying in the wind. The recurrence of ships in André's drawings is a clue to the fundamental importance of his initial crossing between France and the United States.

After two years at boarding school, André returned to live with his parents, who enrolled him in a New York school. André's schooling was the reason the Schiffrins moved from their apartment on the Upper West Side that overlooked the Hudson River to 75th Street, on the Upper East Side. André's parents wanted him to be in the area of New York where he could attend P.S. 6, which "then as now [was] well known as a safe middle-class enclave within the school system."[57] But, as the Schiffrins discovered, it was often difficult to decipher the school boundary maps, and André found himself attending not P.S. 6, but a notoriously bad school, which he would leave a year later to attend the Friends Seminary, a Quaker school, located on East 16th Street. At Friends, André met a large number of children of refugees:

> I was far from the only European refugee child in the school. There were many others, but we never noticed or talked about it. We were all firmly on the path to Americanization, and I realized only much later that, for example, in the class ahead of me was Clem Zimmer, the son of Heinrich Zimmer, a noted German expert on Indian art and philosophy. Another of my classmates was Christian Wolff, son of Helen and Kurt Wolff, who had taken my father on as partner at Pantheon Books.[58]

While Jacques saw himself as an exile, often having discussions with European friends from the past, his son André was being "Americanized." At home, André spoke French. At school, with his friends, he spoke English. Although he was growing up as a young American, reading Disney comic books and passionately following boxing matches, André Schiffrin nevertheless grew up in a unique environment.

To his parents, André was the source of endless joy and hope for the future. In a letter to André Gide in January 1944, Jacques Schiffrin wrote,

> So what can I tell you about us? Our only joy, our only reason for living is Minouche. (André, now: He is proud to carry the same name as you. As I've told you in almost all my letters, he talks

about you often, to everyone: to his school friends, explaining who
you are, etc. He absolutely wants to read your *Interviews*. When
I told him it was too difficult for him, he replied, "Well! Then I'll
wait for it to be published in English [he reads English better
than French]. It is certainly very interesting, and I *must* read what
Monsieur Gide has written.") He's an adorable child. Very sensitive, gifted, intelligent. He gives us nothing but joy.[59]

André's vivacity and intelligence were also evident in a letter
that his mother, Simone, wrote to her sister in July 1945:

He's tall, strong and so intelligent that it stuns people, like Souvarine, who invites him over to discuss the Bible. For two years now,
he has a knowledge and love of the Bible, which he has abandoned only a little out of his interest in politics. He has a critical
nature when it comes to religion, which he discusses with wisdom
and knowledge, but which is counterbalanced, fortunately, by a
great love of painting and his innate creativity. He has written
several poems that were published in a little French review. He
also paints, and his paintings are extraordinary. For the moment,
we are listening, watching. It's very difficult to be the parents of
such a child. For the moment, we adore him, and everything is
going very well. He reads, listens to the radio, goes to museums,
if he feels like it. He discusses everything with his father who has
finally found a worthy opponent. As for me, I laugh. He can hold
his own in a discussion. But I don't get involved in that. While he
finds me very courageous and brave, he also thinks I'm a bit "innocent." But I must stop; once I start talking about my son, I could
go on forever. He's ten now.[60]

Reading these letters, it is obvious that André's parents had
boundless admiration for their child, who brought them happiness in their often painful situation as exiles.

Very early on, André Schiffrin seemed to have a calling to and love for literature. His father emphasized this in a letter to Gide in July 1944:

> Minouche is away at "camp" for two months. These American camps are wonderful. But Minouche writes to us and says he is "terribly lonely" without us, and that he doesn't really like life at camp, because of the sports. "I am going to be a writer, and I don't need to play sports. And I don't like sports." Which means that he needs life at camp more than anyone.[61]

But André Schiffrin's literary standards were influenced by the American milieu in which he was growing up, something that did not necessarily please his father. While he was away at camp in July 1947, Jacques Schiffrin wrote to his son, "I am rather surprised that you write properly, since your main source of reading is comic books and magazines that are not exactly elegant examples of style . . . are they? But, I am not worried. . . . I am sure you prefer Dickens and Victor Hugo to Nancy and Mickey."[62]

André Schiffrin was constantly shifting between popular American culture, in which he was immersed, and the demands of European literature, which his father sought to pass on to him. He seems to have achieved a certain symbiosis, since it is in the language he mastered best, English, that he wrote to Gide, the "major contemporary figure," to tell him, on May 6, 1946, "I cannot wait till I can read your books."[63] And in April 1948, Gide very affectionately wrote directly to Minouche, "I really wish that, later on, you will be able to understand and like my books: It seems a little as if I've written them for you."[64] The wonderful relationship begun through letters between the two Andrés would soon become concrete.

Their plan to meet would take shape in 1949. Jacques still wanted to return to France, but his health prevented it. Jacques wrote to Gide that Simone intended to go to France in the summer, perhaps with Minouche.[65] In the end, André went alone. At the beginning of May, everything was arranged, and Gide exclaimed, "Your excellent letter of May 5 sent me head over heels, and fills my heart with great joy: I'll see my friend Minouche again. Unbelievable. I had barely dared to hope. I'm as happy as if I were his age."[66] From then on, they organized and prepared the trip. It was not easy for a fourteen-year-old to cover such a great distance alone. But Jacques Schiffrin saw Gide as a brother with whom he could entrust his Minouche for part of his French adventure.[67]

In this new and unusual situation—an adventure more than an ordeal—Gide was again present, coming to the aid of the Schiffrin family. When discussing the possibility of André taking a ship to Algiers, then to Marseille, Gide said that he would contact his friend, the poet Jean Amrouche, who had relatives living in Algiers. In Marseille, Gide said (in his best English) that he would find "the wright man."[68] Afterwards, Minouche would go as quickly as possible to Gide, who would be expecting him in Nice. It had been nearly ten years since the two Andrés had seen each other, so Gide asked Schiffrin for a photo of his son. The publisher sent him one in May 1949, along with a magnificent description of his son, a portrait worth quoting at length:

Here is a photo of André. It's an old one (two or three years), but I don't have any more recent ones. He looks a little delicate in this photo. But not a bit of it: He's a tall, strong lad and behaves impeccably (touch wood). You wanted a description. Here we go: above all, very intelligent and spiritual. Very cheerful. An ability to be endlessly enthralled. Generous. A great deal of charm. Brilliant conversationalist (not in French, alas, but in English).

His primary passion (apart from stamp collecting): politics. Devours an enormous quantity of newspapers, magazines, reviews, listens to the radio; reads all sorts of political writing. Better informed about current events (both national and international) than your average American congressman. After politics, psychology. But very childlike, able to amuse himself with an electric train. Never bored. Likes to be alone and definitely prefers the company of adults (he's going to be fourteen in three weeks). Faults: terribly lazy, especially physically. Likes no sport at all, not even walking. Unbelievably careless, gourmand (and gourmet). Weighs seven or eight kilos more than me (though it's true I weigh nothing), loves ice cream, cakes, chocolates, honey, etc. incapable of resisting, doesn't give a d . . . about getting fat. Do you remember that you found he had an astonishing sense of humor for a child of three (Cuverville, 1938)? He hasn't lost that. Quite the contrary. He is very funny, and nothing comical escapes him. Our relationship is excellent, VERY LITTLE like father and son. He has an idiotic admiration for me that I fight in vain. Mostly calls me Yacha, or "my dear" (same with Simone, with whom he is in love, and rightly so). When he goes to his room in the evening (goes to bed around 12:00, 12:30), he says, "Good night, my dears," and feels he is very much our protector. A great deal of common sense and good sense. Seriously influenced by American-style "business." So that is a portrait as good as I can paint. Are parents capable of objective judgment? I think I am. You will tell me if I'm right. He hasn't read any of your works; "What can I read by Gide?"—"Nothing yet."[69]

This beautiful portrait revealed not only a young boy with a promising, brilliant future, but also a father at once loving and devoted but also concerned with his son's future and wary of the American influence on his education.

At the end of May, André Schiffrin left for France. The journey would last two months. Simone and Jacques would pay a mere $50 toward the trip. For the rest of his stay, the family had to count on their friends and relatives for both the cost of the voyage and living expenses once there. To pay for the trip by boat, the Schiffrins took advantage of their cordial relationship with the Dreyfus family, who owned an important grain export business based in the United States. Thanks to the Dreyfus family, André was able to get passage and a free berth on a small cargo boat.[70] The ship left from Philadelphia, where Simone accompanied her son. Nearly nine years after leaving Marseille, André Schiffrin was again on a transatlantic crossing, heading for the land where he was born. Three weeks later, André arrived in Caen, in Normandy. André's return to France greatly impressed him:

> Thus my first look at Europe was a shocking one: Caen had been badly bombed in 1944 during the liberation, and even by the time of my landing five years later it was still largely in ruins. The area around the port was completely flattened, and the town center had very few buildings standing. I hadn't expected anything like this. The American press had given no indication that Europe was still so shattered. I proceeded through the devastation to the Paris train, badly shaken by this first view of what the war had meant to France.[71]

In Paris, André Schiffrin stayed with an old friend of his father's: Louis Martin-Chauffier, a journalist, writer, and member of the Resistance who had been captured by the Germans and sent to a concentration camp. As André Schiffrin later wrote,

> In many ways, his apartment reflected his own appearance. He [Martin-Chauffier] was tired, worn out, having never recovered

from his Calvary. One of the first things I did upon my return to New York was to read his memoir, and then all the others I could find, such as David Rousset's classic but now forgotten *The Other Kingdom*, Primo Levi's *If This Is a Man*, and the others that described the experience that could so easily have been my family's.[72]

His journey to France and interaction with Martin-Chauffier gave André a profound understanding of the causes of his parents' departure, the threat that hung over them, and the reasons they escaped by crossing the Atlantic.

In Paris, André walked everywhere, from Pigalle to Trocadéro, and visited members of his family, including his aunt Bella and her husband, Serge, who took him to see *Les Halles*, the city's central market. He also went to the rue de l'Université, where his family had lived until their apartment was requisitioned by the Germans. However, it was one thing to visit family and to rediscover the places where he had lived as a child but quite another to meet the Gallimards.

Jacques Schiffrin had asked his son to pay a visit to his former employers, which he did. As André Schiffrin recalls,

> My father had asked me to visit Gallimard, the publishing house to whom he had sold his *Pléiade* series and where he had worked during his last years in France. After the war, of course, he had hoped to return to his old job, but the Gallimards had filled his position and made it clear that there would be no room for him. So my visit was, at best, delicate and fraught.

Afterward, he wrote to his parents, describing his visit to Gallimard: "Very rich, full of Gallimards, but very businesslike, very cold and very sad. I shook a lot of hands, everyone asked how my father was, but it's impossible to tell you whether they were really interested or just being polite."[73]

Times had truly changed. The warmth that Jacques Schiffrin might have felt at Gallimard before the war no longer existed. Strangely enough, it was around this time, at the beginning of summer 1949, that Jacques Schiffrin wrote to Raymond Gallimard once again to ask him if it would be possible to find a place for him in the publishing house. Under the circumstances, André Schiffrin's trip might also be seen as a test, giving him the opportunity to observe the situation on the ground, as well as to see whether André might like living in Paris. In addition to his visit to Gallimard, Gaston invited André to have lunch with him at his large apartment overlooking the Palais-Royal Garden in Paris. André Schiffrin had only good memories of their lunch: "In any case, he invited me to lunch in his apartment and did so very kindly. I can remember no awkward pauses in our conversation, although I should note that my father had not told me of the series of problems that had started when Gallimard had dismissed him a mere nine years before."[74]

Having walked all through Paris and fulfilled his mission at Gallimard, André Schiffrin was able to continue his journey in the footsteps of his father by going to the South of France, where Jacques's great friends—André Gide and Roger Martin du Gard—were waiting for him.

André Gide was expecting the publisher's son at his villa in Juan-les-Pins sometime after July 17.[75] On July 20, Gide wrote to Jacques Schiffrin, describing his enthusiasm for his son after Minouche had arrived:

So he is finally here, the one I've been eagerly waiting for; he's been here for two days; my astonishment at seeing him is far from diminished. I could almost say, quite the contrary; for I have only gradually been discovering the extraordinary maturity of this child who is still so young; and which, at first, out of a kind of modesty, he rather sought to hide rather than boast of it, or even allow it to be seen. . . . We would be cheated, my dear friend, if he did not become someone both remarkable and remarked (and rather quickly so that we might, me as well, rejoice in it).[76]

Jacques Schiffrin, extremely happy and touched by Gide's impressions of his son, nonetheless remained fearful that the American culture in which André had grown up might steer him toward a destiny less dignified than he had hoped. Speaking of the Americans, he wrote, "They don't understand the necessity of going to the sources. I often have difficulty in explaining that to André. I am quite frightened that he may use all his gifts as a journalist. His talents would be wasted. But perhaps he would also be happier."[77] By having André cross the Atlantic, Jacques Schiffrin was seeking to familiarize him with the French culture Jacques Schiffrin dreamed of and which André Gide incarnated. With Gide, in Juan-les-Pins, André Schiffrin could observe the writer at work amid his admirers.

On July 22, André Schiffrin left Gide to spend a day with his father's other great friend, Roger Martin du Gard, who told André to meet him in Nice, at the Place Masséna, in front of the large door to the casino. André took a bus from Juan-les-Pins, and Martin du Gard gave the young André some details so he could easily recognize him: "An old man with white hair. Grey waistcoat. Coarse white trousers, who will patiently wait, as long as necessary."[78]

The next day, Martin du Gard described André's visit in a letter to Jacques Schiffrin. They had walked all over Nice together in constant conversation:

[André] very sweetly was interested in everything, or pretended to be with endless good grace. We chatted about everything, and . . . I found him extraordinarily level headed, sensible, thoughtful for his age, like a child used to living surrounded by adults, and who already has attained the wisdom to adapt to circumstances. . . . His love for you and your wife is obvious every time he speaks of you and your difficult American existence. I can sense that your trio is exceptionally close, and I understand the place this child must hold in both your lives. He always returns to you; and in the pleasure he finds in discovering new things, I believe that what matters the most is for him to be able to discuss those things with you when he returns. At five thirty, I put him back on the bus for Juan-les-Pins, and we said good-bye to each other like old friends.[79]

André also retained excellent memories of the day he spent with Roger Martin du Gard:

[He] was very different from Gide, warm and friendly, and very approachable, known for his welcoming smile and total lack of hauteur. In Nice we walked for hours along the Promenade des Anglais, talking like equals and having a marvelous time together. He seemed determined to show me every aspect of Nice, its harbor and still-lovely old city. The walk was nothing for me—I was used to crossing Paris by then—and of course it didn't occur to me that Martin du Gard was by then an old man. I felt I'd met a true friend.[80]

If this trip made André a kind of ambassador of Jacques's in France, it also allowed the publisher to introduce a fundamental element of his life to friends who had remained in France. More than all the letters exchanged, André's visit to France was a concrete way to send news and allow people to understand the life the Schiffrins led in New York, their problems as well as their great pride and joy, this child with endless curiosity.

Once back in Juan-les-Pins, André accompanied Gide to Avignon, where the writer was attending the premiere of his play *Pasiphaë* at the Festival d'Avignon. Awed by the performance of the play in the courtyard of the Palais des Papes, André became aware of the place his father's friend held in the French literary world. Amid his admirers, Gide seemed so "distant from ordinary mortals."[81] From Avignon, André went to Marmande, where, filled with memories of his new friends, he spent a month with Simone's younger sister, Paulette.

Upon his return to New York in September, after a three-week trip by sea from Rouen to Philadelphia, André Schiffrin wrote to Gide. At school again, he fell back into his routine, but he assured André Gide that he would never forget the week spent in his company: "Again I thank you for a 'wonderful time' and the week that I shall remember all my life, and surely tell to my grandchildren."[82]

When André Schiffrin embarked from Philadelphia in the summer of 1949, it was not yet clear that Jacques Schiffrin would never see Paris again. Thus, André's trip reminded the Parisian literary microcosm that on the other side of the Atlantic, one of their own was still alive and that he would like to see the Seine once more. In addition to this professional matter, André allowed Jacques to cement a link with individuals whose friendships were challenged by his exile but which he did everything possible to retain. The fact that his son got along well with Gide and Martin du Gard was a source of infinite happiness and pride for Jacques Schiffrin. The trip was also a rite of passage, the handing down of a heritage from father to son. To Jacques, it was essential that his son understand his roots, to discover both the literary world his father had been a part of and France, the country that had made him a citizen, where he had met André's mother, where he had been happy. And of course, André had to understand the reality of what the war had meant. By meeting the Martin-Chauffier family and Jacques's half-sister, Bella, whose mother had been deported and killed, André could understand the tragedy that lay at the heart of his family's departure, the horror that explained his first transatlantic crossing, and perhaps, to a certain extent, his parents' sadness.

Jacques Schiffrin's desire to pass down his heritage seemed to bear fruit. André would never forget his father's writer friends or the love of literature that Jacques wished to pass on to him. He would even make it his career, taking on the same role as his father: a publisher. And André would never forget his roots, the France where he had been born in 1935, profoundly transformed by the war, and which he would rediscover for the first time in the summer of 1949. Soon, André's life would be full of journeys between Paris and New York.

FINAL HOPES

André's trip was a breath of fresh air for Jacques Schiffrin, given that the last years of his life were marked by a great deal of disillusionment. His final hopes of returning, and of reuniting with the friends he had left nearly ten years before coming to New York, faded away.

The major question of 1948 was whether Gide would cross the Atlantic and come to New York City. As Schiffrin could not return to Paris, perhaps his close friend—the man who had literally saved his life—could come to New York. At least, this was what Gide hinted to his friend: "It is highly likely that I will

make a visit to the U.S. in the spring, accompanied by Pierre
Herbart (one conference in Baltimore; two months' stay in Florida). Wonderful chance to see you again (but keep it quiet!!),
which would make me so very happy."[83] Schiffrin could not con-
ceal his delight: "God! What a joy that would be for me, for us
all. A greater joy than you could ever imagine!"[84] Schiffrin would
thus have the immense pleasure of seeing the person who had
emotionally accompanied him throughout his long American
odyssey. To Schiffrin, Gide symbolized not only France, Paris,
and his intellectual life, but Russia as well, the Russia he had
rediscovered in the company of his friend in 1936, when the
two colleagues were immersed in their joint translations. But,
ultimately, Gide, who was seventy-eight in 1948, was no longer
strong enough to undertake such a journey. Like Schiffrin, he
was too old. In 1948, both were exhausted. The bad news from
Gide arrived in April:

> I had to give up the idea of coming to America just as I could not
> go to Sweden. This is very painful for me as I was overjoyed at the
> idea of seeing all three of you. I can't think about it! Incognito
> impossible (just been named Doctor Honoris Causa at Columbia
> University!) and much too tired.[85]

To Schiffrin, it was a harsh blow: "To describe how disappointed
we were, Simone and I, when we learned of your decision to
abandon your trip to the United States is beyond my literary
capability! I had organized everything to accompany you to
Florida. . . . Alas! It is in God's hands, and we all know that
things do not always work to our advantage!"[86]

If Schiffrin could not become a publisher in Paris again, if it
were impossible to have a position at Gallimard, why not rein-
vent himself? As early as May 1947, he dreamed of spending his

last years in Southern France.[87] Schiffrin's final hope for a return to France was part of an impossible dream: to open a small bookstore in Nice, where he could live between Gide and Martin du Gard. In one of the letters Raymond Gallimard sent Schiffrin just after the war, he mentioned what had happened to some of the people who had once worked at the publishing house: "Mme Gras has left us (I think you were still here then) to take over a bookstore in Nice."[88] In 1949, when Jacques Schiffrin proposed this project, perhaps he was recalling his former colleague and hoped that he, too, might start a new life on the French Riviera. Schiffrin spoke about his plan to Gide in June 1949:

I had the idea of going to Nice and setting up a bookstore. (Perhaps publishing one or two books a year.) What do you think? Please do me the favor of telling me how you feel about that idea. Do the Bussys live in Nice? Perhaps they could give me some tips? And Roger Martin du Gard, whom I'm writing to now as well. His presence there has influenced my choice a great deal. I think that French publishers (including Hachette) would make things easy for me, even if only at the beginning (starting over again once more! Would this be the last time? If only Aragon could become King of France. . . .) Please: Reply, as soon as you can, about my idea—a bookstore in Nice—and give me news of your health.[89]

The Bussys were Dorothy and Simon Bussy, close friends of Gide; she was a novelist, he a painter, and they lived near Nice. With the bookstore idea, Schiffrin had not given up hope of publishing; he wanted to continue but in a reduced way, perhaps bringing out the unpublished works of André Gide. If a return to Paris and Gallimard was blocked by the new literary order that reigned in a Paris from which Jacques Schiffrin seemed

excluded, why not establish himself as a bookseller on the Promenade des Anglais in Nice? Jacques Schiffrin also mentioned the
possible support of Hachette, which was then directed by his old
friend Henri Filipacchi.

Filipacchi, who knew Schiffrin well from working alongside
him on the *Éditions de la Pléiade*, seemed enthusiastic about
the idea:

> I would not usually advise anyone to start up as a bookseller, for
> there are three times as many than before the war. But there is no
> longer a single real bookstore, and in just a week, you, my dear
> Jacques, would become the best bookseller in Nice or Cannes
> or anywhere. I guarantee you'd make a good living. I doubt any-
> one makes millions in that profession, but that's not what you're
> expecting, is it? I repeat that in spite of all the beautiful boutiques,
> there is an essential one that is missing: a bookstore! The profes-
> sion is run by morons, so much so that I have begun to hate it. But
> you, you would succeed.[90]

Some of Schiffrin's other old friends were more doubtful.
To Gide and Martin du Gard, the idea of opening a bookstore
in Nice was "idealistic and rash," as Gide wrote to Schiffrin.[91]
In June 1949, Gide and Martin du Gard discussed the most
appropriate response to Schiffrin's idea. Martin du Gard wrote
to Gide,

> Dear friend, forgive me, but I really can't reply to Schiffrin with-
> out consulting you. Especially as he has probably already asked
> your advice, and we mustn't keep him sitting on the fence. . . .
> Should we encourage him to return to this absurd Europe?
> And especially to France? And particularly to Nice?? What would
> he do? What bitter bread awaits him?

Nice is heaven for people of "independent means"; but, to my knowledge, a "terrible" place to earn a living. The businessmen in Nice stick together and exclude foreigners, even if they are French. Gangsters & Co. S[chiffrin]'s only skill, and it is a very great one, I think, is publishing. But in Nice, out of the question to publish. . . . A bookstore? But thirty new ones have sprung up since '45, and they are stagnating, not just as they are everywhere, but more than anywhere; for if the book trade is the first to suffer from the lack of personal resources, it is in Nice that people make the least sacrifices to be cultured. In Nice, it is digests and celebrity magazines that sell the most.

And as sensitive as he is (I love him a great deal, but I am not blind to his weaknesses), if we dissuade him from this madness, he will think we don't want him to return and that we prefer to keep him at a distance.[92]

The final argument was the financial question. It was this aspect that Martin du Gard stressed when he wrote to Schiffrin on July 4, 1949, to discourage him:

A bookstore? But the sale of books has been affected more than any other business. People are so constrained by their budgets that the first thing they economize on is books. I see very cultured people who hardly read anymore and aren't buying now, because they can't. In the last four years, in Nice, as in Paris, we've seen a heap of small bookstores open, which stagnate for one or two years and then go bankrupt. The ones that survive are always the ones that, in the past, were book clubs with a stock of books it loaned to its subscribers. But how, at current prices, could a book club be formed?

The plan to open a bookstore in Nice would only be possible if an established publishing house, or bookstore, from Paris, decided to open a branch in the Midi, and would offer that you manage

it, with a fixed salary, and without any personal risk. What Gaston did with Roland Saucier, on the Boulevard Raspail. But given
the current financial crisis, I strongly doubt that any publishing
house of that type would wish to commit the large sums of capital
necessary to start such an uncertain business, in order to have any
chance of fighting the competition that already exists.[93]

Martin du Gard was being realistic. Schiffrin's dream did not
take into account the reality of the sums involved or the global
economic situation. Immediately after the war, French society
had not yet recovered or entered the consumer age. The country
was still emerging from the war, and its economic difficulties were
obvious. It was an economic obstacle that made Henri Filipacchi
somewhat doubtful about Jacques Schiffrin's plan for a business
in Nice, which he relayed to Gide but not directly to Schiffrin,
with whom he remained enthusiastic about the idea: "There is
an important 'but': Filipacchi thinks that to set up a bookstore
would cost at least four to five million francs!!"[94] And Jacques
Schiffrin, given his history with the Gallimards, did not want
to ask Gaston to become the manager of an official Gallimard
bookstore on the banks of the Mediterranean, as Roland Saucier
has become, in Paris, on the Boulevard Raspail.

Jacques Schiffrin's financial situation in New York was far
from enviable and did not allow him to envision investing such
a sum to open a bookstore in Nice on his own. As Gide wrote
to Schiffrin in September 1948, "I fear, my dear friend, that you
have offered terms that are far too advantageous to me, and it
pains me to drive around in a luxurious car paid for by my royalties, while you have to count on your wife's work to make ends
meet."[95] The author even wondered if Schiffrin was being taken
advantage of by his American publishing partners, who did not
fully understand his friend's difficult financial situation. But that

was not the case. Jacques Schiffrin had quite simply sacrificed his material comfort for the editorial quality of the works published by Pantheon. Schiffrin replied in July 1949, "No! I haven't allowed myself to be 'conned' or 'not taken precautions' at Pantheon. We are four 'officers' (administrators) who receive very meager salaries, but who get a share of the profits. But for three years now, there haven't been any."[96] Needless to say, finding millions of francs to open a bookstore in Nice was quite simply out of the question.

In his letter of July 4, 1949, Martin du Gard introduced a more profound argument against opening a bookstore in which he denigrated Jacques Schiffrin's nostalgia:

> All of this seems terribly utopian to me. . . . Be very careful, my dear friend, not to miss sight of the forest for the trees, and to exchange, without serious forethought, the Purgatory of New York for a Hell in Europe. Do not be the victim of a mirage. . . . Get it well into your head that the France you knew and loved no longer exists! "Moscow! . . . Moscow ! . . ." the Three Sisters of Chekhov said over and over again. . . . My heart goes out to you; your nostalgia is *pathetic.*[97]

Martin du Gard, who had always regarded Schiffrin's return to Paris as a fantasy to be discouraged, was no longer trying to console his friend.[98]

In any case, Jacques Schiffrin was far too ill in the summer of 1949 to seriously undertake such an enterprise. In his autobiography, André Schiffrin criticized, in a rare move, the attitude of his father's friends: "Martin du Gard and Gide could have saved their arguments. I now realize that there was really no possibility of my father being allowed to return; they did not realize how ill he was."[99]

JACQUES SCHIFFRIN, JUDAISM,
AND ANDRÉ GIDE

Strongly dissuaded by his close friends, Jacques Schiffrin finally abandoned the temptation to go to Nice. It was undoubtedly his health that prevented him from undertaking such a journey, but his friends' words had also been sufficiently strong to influence him. So Schiffrin remained in New York. He was becoming aware that time was passing, that the possibility of spending his final days in Manhattan was likely. It was necessary to put his affairs in order, to clarify certain things that he had put on hold for years, the kinds of things that prevent friendship from evolving into brotherhood. In October 1949, while re-reading Gide's *Journal*, Schiffrin decided to question his friend on a point that had "always shocked" him. In what is the last known letter that Jacques Schiffrin sent to André Gide, he writes,

The other day, I came across a passage that had always shocked me. (Why haven't I spoken to you about it sooner? God knows.) It is on page 1035, in the *Pléiade* edition. You name a few second- and third-rate writers (several of the names I didn't even know: Coolus, Sternheim) and state that they wrote "Jewish literature, in which any ideas of dignity are lacking. It is demeaning literature." The list could have gone on forever, with names that were not Jewish. That is obvious. But what about Bergson, for example, or Montaigne or Proust (half-Jewish, it's true)? And Heine and Kafka? And Pasternak and Mandelstam? The Russians would be very astonished to learn that their two great poets are "demeaning . . . Jewish literature," etc. Jewish literature is the Bible ("ideas of dignity are lacking"? "demeaning"?) and other writings that neither you nor I know. No, in truth! I find your statement neither very fair nor very responsible.[100]

At first glance, Jacques Schiffrin's relationship to Judaism was rather simple. Born to a Jewish family and named Yakov (Jacob) in Baku, Jacques nevertheless grew up in a secular environment, part of the middle classes of the current capital of Azerbaijan. In his autobiography, André Schiffrin discusses the place of religion in his parents' life:

> My family were typical secularized Jews, opposed to all religions, following none of the rites or customs of Judaism. In Russia, many Jewish intellectuals had considered rabbis to be conveyors of superstition and irrationality. Both of my parents were aware of their origins, of course, but they were among the many in Europe who became Jews because of Hitler.[101]

Jacques Schiffrin, who had partied in Monte Carlo, who was at the heart of Parisian high society between the world wars, and who lived for painting, music, and literature was undoubtedly little concerned with the question of religion. And throughout his life, the question of Zionism never seemed to come up. In the family archives, there is no indication of a religious marriage between Jacques and Simone Schiffrin. Thus, as André Schiffrin indicates, Jacques Schiffrin's Judaism was a result of Hitler's policies. In New York, Kurt Wolff seemed to have followed the same path. So it is not surprising to find within their correspondence the occasional "Mazel Tov!" after some good publishing news.[102]

Schiffrin was very aware of the fate of his fellow Jews and family members who had remained in Europe. Jacques's stepmother, his father's second wife—who was also Jacques's aunt—died in a concentration camp. When the war ended, Schiffrin knew that he would never see many of his relatives again: "[We] barely dare to think about the people we will meet again (or the ones we'll never see again. . . .)," he wrote to Gide in July 1944.[103] Then, in April 1948: "I can't help thinking about the people who were sick and went to the Nazi concentration camps . . . or the Russian ones!"[104] And finally, in a long letter in October 1949: "In Europe, they seem very proud of the culture that led to Dachau, Buchenwald and the Siberian mines. We are very far from Alyosha Karamazov who thought that the suffering of a single child was worth a myriad of planets."[105] The cruelty of people, as witnessed in the tragedy of the Second World War, was endlessly present in Jacques Schiffrin's mind: "Men are monsters," he wrote in his last letter to Gide, referring to the atrocities of recent history.

Gide had to explain himself: How could he judge Jewish literature as demeaning? On October 12, Gide replied to his friend, confirming he had added a few pages to his letter that would clarify his stance on the question: "May they bring you some consolation!"[106] Unfortunately, those pages are not found in the correspondence between Gide and Schiffrin. Alban Cerisier, the editor of the Gide–Schiffrin correspondence, has put forth the hypothesis that the text Gide sent to Schiffrin was the one he wrote after reading Sartre's *Réflexions sur la question juive* (*Anti-Semite and Jew*), published in 1946:

> The thesis presented here [by Sartre] is the same one argued by my friend Schiffrin: The traits that are characteristic of Jews (I mean the ones that you, the anti-Semites, reproach them for) are traits acquired over the centuries, traits that you have forced them to acquire. The long conversation I had with him contained certain arguments that come up again here, and which scarcely surprise me anymore. That conversation today seems more clever and baseless than exact, in spite of the profound and tender affection that I have always had, and which continues to grow, for Schiffrin,

in whom, I must also say, that I saw very little of the faults that might be considered Jewish *defects*, but only their qualities.[107]

Here we learn that Sartre's thesis (that it is anti-Semitism that creates the "Jew") was close to Schiffrin's own position, but it is also possible that André Gide retained essentialist views about Judaism, identifying certain defects or qualities he felt were unique to Jews. It is difficult to know whether Gide's words brought "some consolation" to Jacques Schiffrin. But even if the author was susceptible to the anti-Semitic prejudices of his time, he nevertheless stood alongside Schiffrin throughout his long journey, helping him escape the persecution that awaited him had he remained in France.

Despite the complexities of the issue, Jacques Schiffrin, who had come to identify as Jewish through the force of history, felt the need to clarify this with his old friend, daring to tell him that his statement about Jewish literature was "neither very fair nor very responsible."[108] Waiting any longer to say what he felt would have meant risking never saying it at all. Jacques Schiffrin's health was clearly deteriorating.

THE END OF A LIFE

In 1950, Jacques Schiffrin, turned fifty-eight and was looking gaunt. As André Schiffrin wrote, "The last photos show him looking incredibly thin, very much like the concentration camp survivors we had seen in photographs."[109] At night, Schiffrin could sleep only with oxygen next to his bed. He had smoked all his life and suffered from emphysema, which made it nearly impossible to move: "Going from one room to the next makes me suffocate,"[110] Schiffrin wrote in 1949. In addition to the emphysema, Schiffrin had lung cancer, a fact he did not know when he died but which an autopsy later revealed.[111] Nevertheless, he was fully aware of his poor state of health. As he wrote to Roger Martin du Gard in January 1950, "I had a dreadful winter. One cold after the other, and the slightest cold takes on serious proportions because of my breathing problem. Time is passing quickly, horribly quickly—and as the Russians say, 'Soon it will be the lid.'"[112] Jacques Schiffrin spent every summer in the countryside north of New York City to breathe the clean air in the hope of improving his fragile state of health, but it did no good, and his illness continued to worsen.

In the spring of 1950, Jacques Schiffrin replied to an invitation from Svetlana Alexeïeff, the daughter of his friend Alexandre, who had worked briefly as a secretary at Pantheon Books. She suggested that he spend the summer with her and her husband in Vermont, near Bennington College.[113] Painters and college professors lived nearby, and in the evening, Svetlana held memorable poker games, which Jacques took part in, a drink in hand. But he was extremely weak. Svetlana Alexeïeff particularly remembered the difficulty he had in carrying his suitcases when he arrived at the Albany train station: Any physical exertion had become painful. Jacques slept in the same room as Svetlana's newborn baby. According to his host, Jacques's situation in New York had become complicated, the family atmosphere weighed down by his illness.

In the fall of 1950, Jacques Schiffrin returned to New York. He had work to do at Pantheon and many doctors' visits to attend. In the United States, the beginning of the Korean War and the fear of a new world conflict dominated the news. To Martin du Gard, Schiffrin spoke of his concern over Minouche "who in three to four years could be mobilized (they're starting to get killed at eighteen or nineteen). He also thinks about it a lot. . . . We need a miracle."[114]

Schiffrin also wished to make peace with Boris de Schloezer, a man he considered a brother and with whom he and Gide had translated Alexander Pushkin's *The Queen of Spades* to launch the *Éditions de la Pléiade* in Paris at the beginning of the 1920s. Without explaining the cause of their disagreement, Schiffrin wrote, "Your last letter completely erased the impression of the first one. And I would ask you to excuse my little spitefulness (regarding erudition)."[115] It was doubtlessly nothing of great significance, but in October 1950, it was important for the man that Boris de Schloezer affectionately called Yacha to mend fences with one of his oldest, closest friends.

During this same period, Jacques Schiffrin wrote to Raymond Gallimard about his account. In his letter of November 5, 1940, Gaston Gallimard had stated, "It is our intention, of course, to honor the terms of our contract." Jacques Schiffrin's detailed letter of October 24, 1950, was written to Raymond Gallimard, whom he had met in New York a few months before, in May 1950. Schiffrin asked Raymond Gallimard one last time to "send the money I'm owed," insisting on the fact that "anything would help for someone who earns so little here."[116] This is the last known letter Jacques Schiffrin wrote. It once again bears witness to Schiffrin's difficult financial state of affairs in New York, as well as his desire to clarify the situation with Gallimard. As Svetlana Alexeïeff emphasized, Schiffrin was "haunted" by the brutal break of his association with Gallimard.[117] Feeling his strength diminish, it seems he wished to sort out his legal issues with Gallimard, in particular requesting information about his accounts for the period from 1940 to 1945, as well as the amount he was owed in 1950. On November 10, 1950, Raymond

Gallimard, "somewhat surprised" by Jacques's letter, replied.[118] To Raymond Gallimard, the agreement between the publishing house and Jacques Schiffrin was of a different kind:

> I recall having detailed for you . . . the solution I envisaged, which then seemed, and still seems appropriate, satisfactory to you, agreeable to everyone, and, moreover, constructed so as to avoid either of us the necessity of having to interpret contracts that are unclear for me, and for the company, for the allocation of rather complicated accounts and discussions that would be cruel and lacking in warmth.
>
> This solution, produced in a climate of pure friendship, which seemed to be agreeable to you, was as follows:
>
> From a date to be decided, the Company, in consideration of your valuable contribution, undertakes, as full and final payment of the contracts concluded between the company and yourself, to pay you a flat annual fee, the amount to be decided, for the rest of your life. . . . The Company proposes to place at your disposal five hundred thousand francs a year (500,000), for the rest of your life, beginning on June 30, 1949.[119]

Thus, every year until his death, Schiffrin would receive the sum of 500,000 francs, which was twice as much as he had received until then according to contracts that were difficult to decipher. This arrangement might have seemed relatively advantageous to the publisher. However, he never had the chance to reply to Raymond Gallimard's final offer. He died before his dispute with Gallimard was resolved.

On November 10, Jacques Schiffrin was admitted to the Polyclinic Hospital in the East Village. This hospital, formerly the German Dispensary, had opened at the end of the nineteenth century to care for German immigrants who had come to live in New York, in particular on the southeast side of Manhattan. When he went into the hospital, it was to have a procedure to help his breathing. But the procedure led to serious complications, leaving Schiffrin in a critical state. The surgeons at the Polyclinic operated on him for a collapsed lung. Simone was at his side, and the operation was a success. "He was resuscitated,"[120] Simone wrote to Boris de Schloezer. Schiffrin no longer needed an oxygen tent and was able to sit up in bed and could speak. But it soon became apparent that the operation was only delaying the inevitable. Further tests revealed that Jacques Schiffrin's condition was still critical. According to Simone, on November 17, shortly before two o'clock in the morning, Jacques Schiffrin died "suddenly."[121]

The numerous moving testimonies and speeches that followed his death form a memorable portrait of the publisher who, from Paris to New York, had left an indelible mark on the worlds of literature and culture. Simone received many letters of condolence and wrote a few words to their closest family and friends. Some of them, like Kurt Wolff and Hermann Broch, made public speeches paying homage to their friend.

On November 25, Roger Martin du Gard wrote to Jacques Schiffrin's widow from Nice:

> Martin-Chauffier[122] wrote me a note that I found when I returned from Cabris, telling me the terrible news, and I can no longer think of anything else. I will never see my dear Schiffrin again! I now feel suddenly, brutally and absurdly deprived of our long affection for one another, which years of separation had not changed, and on which I had continued to count as a promise for the future, a promise that was postponed but certain.[123]

Roger Martin du Gard, with whom Jacques Schiffrin had corresponded throughout his American adventure, was fully conscious of the difficulties the publisher had faced: "I think of you, of your pain, of your great distress in that large foreign country (where he always felt he was in exile) among new acquaintances, and far from the old, faithful friends that your husband made in France".[124]

Svetlana Alexeïeff also wrote to Simone: "This is the first time in my life that a death means something both close and deeply distressing to me."[125]

André Gide's reaction to Jacques Schiffrin's death, as described by Julien Green in his *Journal*, sums up the ties that united Gide to his close friend, as well as his relationship to Judaism. As Green wrote on November 22, 1950,

> Gide seems very weary. Circles under his eyes, a blank look in his eyes, very pale cheeks and purplish lips (his heart?). He told me almost immediately that Schiffrin had died, which saddened me greatly. Died of what? Then a strange medical term. He couldn't breathe. "He was the only Jew I held in my affection," Gide told me.[126]

André Gide also expressed his "profound sadness" to Simone, stating that his "friendship for him was as strong as if I had just left him yesterday." And Gide again offered to help Simone and André. In a brief message written to Minouche, Gide said of Jacques, "No one deserved to be loved more than he."[127] The last line of Gide's *Journal*, which he had scrupulously kept since 1887, five years before Jacques Schiffrin was born, is dedicated to the death of his friend. On November 21, 1950, Gide wrote, "I have learned (from Mme Martin-Chauffier) that dear Schiffrin has died."[128] And this would be how Gide ended his *Journal*: its final line dedicated to Schiffrin.

In the letter that Simone Schiffrin wrote to Gide, she did not fail to warmly thank the man who had stood by her husband throughout his life. Moreover, Simone reminded him of Jacques's sense of happiness that Gide had been able to meet and appreciate his son André:

> I believe that the fact that you met André was a great joy for Schiffrin, and the letter you wrote him after getting to know André so well was one of the things that made him very happy and very proud.
>
> Please allow me, dear Gide, to thank you for that and for everything you have given him in life.
>
> It was a great deal, and I remain your very grateful,
>
> Simone Schiffrin[129]

Simone Schiffrin also received a letter from Wolfgang Sauerlander, Jacques's colleague at Pantheon, who wrote that Jacques was "a man whom I greatly admired."[130]

On November 20, Raymond Gallimard sent a few words in a telegram: "Terribly sorry, thinking of you sadly and affectionately."[131] And on January 1, 1951, Simone Schiffrin replied to him, without any resentment: "Raymond, let me thank you once again for everything you meant to Jacques during his life and especially at the end of his life when we were so close and you knew us so well." Raymond Gallimard undoubtedly grew closer to the Schiffrins during his time in New York in May 1950, but it seems that she was also committed to defending the interests of Jacques's heirs, as Simone continues, "As for me, I could not start [the year] better knowing, through Simon, that André and I can count on the friendship you had for Jacques and that we could not have any better defenders of our interests."[132]

Jacques's memory was a matter of honor, as well as a practical consideration, aimed at ensuring that André, who was then

fifteen, could continue his studies. Jacques's friends were concerned about the education of their friend's son, and André Gide
and Henri Filipacchi suggested establishing an educational trust
for André.[133]

From Paris, Simone also received messages from members
of Jacques's family, including Bella, his half-sister. Simon Schiffrin, Jacques's brother, who was often in New York, was also in
constant contact with Simone and André and often served as
a go-between between the family and the Gallimard publishing house. Jacques's sister Lyolene, who had taken in the Schiffrins in New York on August 20, 1941, also frequently made the
journey from her home in Kansas City to New York; Simone
described her as "unbelievably loving, kind and courageous."[134]
Boris de Schloezer, to whom Simone described the final days of
Jacques's life, wrote to express his relief at having reconciled with
Jacques shortly before he died: "The only consolation in my distress is that our last exchange of letters was very affectionate and
cleared up a ridiculous misunderstanding that happened without us even knowing why. . . . Was Yacha not a brother to me, a
brother I chose?"[135] Telegrams and messages poured in, in English and French, from Paris and New York. From the two continents, friends born in Russia, France, and the United States sent
Simone Schiffrin words expressing what Jacques Schiffrin had
meant to them and how he had left an impression on them.[136]

A few days after Jacques Schiffrin died, a remembrance service was organized at the Bollingen Foundation in New York,
attended by Jacques's friends and colleagues from Pantheon.
Hermann Broch, the author of *The Sleepwalkers*, which Schiffrin
had published in New York, spoke these words:

> Humanist *pur sang*, that's what he was, and that's what led him
> to the realm where the human spirit appears in its clearest form:

He had to engage himself with books, with art; he had no other choice. His profession was his call. And exactly as he couldn't stand any kind of human uncleanness, he was in revolt against everything he felt as a deprivation of art. He had a kind of sixth sense for detecting lies in art, and when he detected them he became the sharpest, the most merciless critic.

But when he felt the striving for truth in a piece of art, immediately he became a friend, indulgent of every weakness, a helper to overcome difficulties, a fervent co-author full of kindness. His friendship then became productive, and whoever was honored by him in this way never will forget his kind of cooperation, in which he became a true and therefore even tyrannical servant of the work. Here all his skepticism disappeared, and almost passionately his belief in life and its values became visible. His faith made him a skeptic, but his skepticism lead to the presentiment of a new faith, which is bound to come when mankind will survive. He was in his deepest a forerunner, an avant-gardist, but he also made the mistake of being a forerunner in death.[137]

Kurt Wolff also gave homage to the man with whom he had established Pantheon Books. Wolff's homage was more personal, recounting Schiffrin's journey and his suffering at being in exile:

Faced with the tragedy of Jacques Schiffrin's death, a word of Péguy came to my mind: "*On ne meurt pas de sa maladie, on meurt de toute sa vie.*" A man does not die of his illness alone; he dies of his whole life. A week before his death, Jacques said to a friend, "I died ten years ago." And this was true. Jacques was not only victim of his illness, he was also a victim of our cruel times.

For a being as sensitive as he was, the happenings of the last decade in Europe and France were something he could not accept. They haunted him, though personally he had escaped their most dire consequences. When Jacques Schiffrin had to leave his beloved France, something in him died—his joy in living and, as a consequence, his will to live.

With France he left an intellectual life of which he had formed an integral part. He left friends, to whom he was deeply attached: Gide, Malraux, Martin du Gard, Schloezer, and many others, his colleagues in the publishing field, his musician friends, the craftsmen he had been working with—all the ties accumulated through nearly half a century.

Much as he appreciated the liberty and protection he enjoyed in America, he was not able to readjust himself fully to the New World. It was always touching and revealing to see him revive, if only for a brief period, with every visitor from France, with every link with the past.

How happy and excited he was last year when he had the opportunity to send André to France. . . . Yet he did not, as so many other French expatriates, return to France after the war. Europe, for him, had too many dreadful memories; he no longer trusted it. He trusted America.[138]

Kurt Wolff emphasized that Jacques Schiffrin "was not short of friends in his new life, as the current gathering demonstrates" and returned to Schiffrin's influence with his role at Pantheon. The man whose journey was similar to Schiffrin's stressed Jacques's suffering in the New World and the horrible break of ten years earlier owing to his forced departure from France. November 10, 1950, was almost ten years to the day since Jacques Schiffrin received Gaston Gallimard's letter dismissing the *Pléiade*'s creator.

On Schiffrin's death certificate,[139] issued by the Polyclinic Hospital of New York, one question asks, "Of what country was deceased a citizen at time of death?" The initial response was "stateless." This word was then crossed out and corrected with "France." "Stateless" was perhaps how Jacques Schiffrin felt during the final years of his life. It was too soon for him to be recognized as an American citizen but too late for him to feel completely French after having been forced to flee that country, which had revealed its cruelty. Russian? This was undoubtedly the world of the past to Jacques Schiffrin, who had a great sentimental attachment to the country but could not align himself with Stalin's USSR. Thus, "stateless" was crossed out and replaced with "France," the country that had made him a naturalized citizen in 1927, where he had met his wife, where his son had been born, and where he was an acknowledged success. It is therefore understandable that a few months after his death, Jacques Schiffrin's ashes were taken from the Riverside Chapel in New York and transferred to the Père Lachaise cemetery in Paris, the city he had loved so much.

EPILOGUE

L
ike many who fled to the United States during World War II, Schiffrin wished to return to France once the conflict had ended. Yet he was never to return.

The various questions raised by Jacques Schiffrin's journey lived on after him. The challenges posed by the forced displacement of entire populations became a central theme in the twentieth century. On December 14, 1950, a few short weeks after Jacques Schiffrin died, the Office of the United Nations High Commissioner for Refugees was created under the auspices of the United Nations within the framework of the Geneva Convention to address the status of refugees.

Jacques Schiffrin's vision for book publishing also survived him. In 1962, his son André took over as managing director of Pantheon Books. He maintained the tradition of excellence and quality initiated by his father and Kurt Wolff, publishing works by Michel Foucault, Marguerite Duras, Noam Chomsky, Julio Cortázar, and Eric Hobsbawm, among other notable authors.[1] In 1990, Random House, the enormous conglomerate that had recently bought Pantheon Books, forced André Schiffrin out of his position in the name of cutting costs, despite the fact that André Schiffrin's publishing house had met the financial criteria set out by its corporate owner.[2] In 1992, André Schiffrin launched the New Press, where he published authors with whom he had worked at Pantheon, and where he tirelessly continued the family tradition.

André Schiffrin's loyalty to his father's work is evident in the Schiffrin family history. In the late 1950s, André, then a student at Cambridge, where he continued his higher studies thanks to his brilliant academic record at Yale, contacted a Parisian lawyer to examine the terms of his father's dismissal by Gallimard and the nonpayment of the accounts due to Jacques Schiffrin from the *Éditions de la Pléiade*, which Gaston Gallimard had promised to address in his letter of November 5, 1940, and which Jacques Schiffrin was still debating with Raymond Gallimard a week before his death. André Schiffrin became his family's advocate, in the name of his father's honor. He never stopped fighting their cause. In 1999, André Schiffrin wrote to Antoine Gallimard, the current director of Gallimard, with the goal of demanding that the truth concerning his father's forced exile be known. In fact, an article in *Le Monde* from December 1, 1996, entitled "1931, the First *Pléiade*" stated, "While the *Pléiade* remained faithful to Jacques Schiffrin's dream, it has been functioning without him for the past fifty years. At the end of 1939, he immigrated to the United States."[3] Yet at the end of 1939, Jacques Schiffrin had been mobilized into the French Army. The Schiffrins left France in 1941 as a persecuted Jewish family.

This was a question of history for André Schiffrin, and a demand for the truth. By contacting Antoine Gallimard after the publication of this article, André Schiffrin was simply fighting for the truth to be known. And it is this truth that is contained in André Schiffrin's autobiography, *A Political Education: Coming of Age in Paris and New York*, and also in the correspondence between Jacques Schiffrin and André Gide published by Gallimard, if we read between the lines.

Jacques Schiffrin's journey is a mixture of history and memory: the history of the Second World War and publishing and the links between Europe and the United States. But it is also the Schiffrin family's history and, more widely, France's relationship to its view of its involvement in the Second World War. Until the end of the twentieth century, the causes of the departure of the creator of the *Pléiade* remained unknown to the general public.

From France, Jacques Schiffrin brought European culture to the United States. From New York, his son, while defending the tradition of quality publishing under some of the most difficult circumstances on both sides of the Atlantic, contributed in allowing France to better understand its past.

NOTES

INTRODUCTION

1. Taline Ter Minassian, "Bakou 1914–1920," in *Villes en guerre*, ed. Philippe Chassaigne and Jean-Marc Largeaud (Paris: Armand Colin, 2004), 17.

2. André Schiffrin, *A Political Education: Coming of Age in Paris and New York* (New York: Melville House, 2007), 20.

3. According to Saveli's youngest daughter, Isabella, her father was probably born in Voronezh (three hundred kilometers south of Moscow) or Mogilev (now in Belarus).

4. Information provided to the author by the Schiffrin family.

5. Information provided to the author by the Schiffrin family.

6. Jacques Schiffrin's school report. Schiffrin family archives, personal archives, New York.

7. André Schiffrin, *A Political Education*, 21.

8. André Schiffrin, *A Political Education*, 22.

9. André Schiffrin, *A Political Education*, 22.

10. Information provided to the author by the Schiffrin family.

11. This is the number of authors published in the collection as of summer 2016, according to the Pléiade website: http://www.gallimard.fr/Divers /Plus-sur-la-collection/Bibliotheque-de-la-Pleiade/(sourcenode) /116027.

12. Alice Kaplan and Philippe Roussin, "A Changing Idea of Literature: la Bibliothèque de la Pléiade," *Yale French Studies* 89 (1996): 237–62.

13. Joëlle Gleize and Philippe Roussin, eds., *La Bibliothèque de la Pléiade. Travail éditorial et valeur littéraire* (Paris: Editions des Archives Contemporaines, coll. "CEP ENS LSH," 2009), 8.

14. The *Pléiade* is also the name of a group of French poets of the sixteenth century that included Ronsard and du Bellay.

15. Kaplan and Roussin, "A Changing Idea of Literature," 238.

16. André Schiffrin, *A Political Education*, 22

17. *La Nouvelle revue française* 240 (September 1933): 279.

18. Kaplan and Roussin, "A Changing Idea of Literature," 240.

19. Mathieu Lindon, "La Pléiade, une histoire en 566 volumes," *Libération*, December 18, 2010, http://next.liberation.fr/culture/2010/12/18/la-pleiade-une-histoire-en-566-volumes_701557.

20. Kaplan and Roussin, "A Changing Idea of Literature," 241.

21. In 1932, the collection *Classical Russian Authors* included thirteen titles, according to Gleize and Roussin, *La Bibliothèque de la Pléiade*, 16.

22. Pierre Assouline, *Gaston Gallimard, un demi-siècle d'édition française* (Paris: Gallimard, 2006), 235.

23. As Alban Cerisier notes in Gleize and Roussin, *La Bibliothèque de la Pléiade*, 32, Racine was actually the second author published in *La Bibliothèque de la Pléiade*, even though he is listed as number five in the catalog.

24. André Schiffrin, "Jacques Schiffrin, éditeur et créateur de la Pléiade," in Gleize and Roussin, *La Bibliothèque de la Pléiade*, 17.

25. Alban Cerisier, "Du point de vue de l'éditeur, la Pléiade en ses murs," in Gleize and Roussin, *La Bibliothèque de la Pléiade*, 33.

26. Assouline, *Gaston Gallimard*, 11. This is a play on the famous statement by Louis XIV, '*L'État, c'est moi*' ("I am the state").

27. André Gide, *Journal*, vol. 2, *1926–1950* (Paris: Gallimard, 1997), xx.

28. Gaston Doumergue to Jacques Schiffrin, March 1, 1927. Bibliothèque littéraire Jacques Doucet, Paris. Don Schiffrin. Ms 51165.

29. André Gide and Edmond Jaloux, *Correspondance: 1896–1950* (Lyon: Presses universitaires de Lyon, 2005), 259.

30. Frank Lestringant, *André Gide, L'Inquiéteur* (Paris: Flammarion, 2012), 606.

31. Regis Debray, foreword to *Emigrés à New York, les intellectuels français à Manhattan, 1940–1944*, by Jeffrey Mehlman (Paris: Albin Michel, 2005), 10.

1. FROM WAR TO EXILE

1. Maria van Rysselberghe, *Les Cahiers de la Petite Dame*, vol. 3 (Paris: Gallimard, 1998), 76.

2. van Rysselberghe, *Les Cahiers*, 109.

3. van Rysselberghe, *Les Cahiers*, 130.

4. Letter from Jacques Schiffrin to Gustavo Gili, November 1939. Schiffrin family archives, personal archives, New York/Correspondence Gili.

5. André Gide and Jacques Schiffrin, *Correspondance, 1922–1950* (Paris: Gallimard, 2005), 117.

6. Gide and Schiffrin, *Correspondance*, 121.

7. Gide and Schiffrin, *Correspondance*, 131.

8. André Gide and Roger Martin du Gard, *Correspondance* (Paris: Gallimard, 1997), 191.

9. Roger Martin du Gard, *Journal*, vol. 3 (Paris: Gallimard, 1993), 322.

10. Gide and Schiffrin, *Correspondance*, 145.

11. Letter from Jacques Schiffrin to Dimitri Snégaroff, February 13, 1940. "Jacques Schiffrin et les éditions de La Pléiade." *Imprimerie Union*. Accessed May 20, 2018. http://imprimerie-union.org/apollinaire-a-maeght /jacques-schiffrin.

12. Letter from Roger Martin du Gard to Jacques Schiffrin, March 11, 1940. Bibliothèque littéraire Jacques Doucet, Paris. Don Schiffrin. Ms Ms 51187.

13. Letter from Jacques Schiffrin to Dimitri Snégaroff, May 12, 1940. "Jacques Schiffrin et les éditions de La Pléiade." *Imprimerie Union*. http://imprimerie-union.org/apollinaire-a-maeght/jacques-schiffrin.

14. Gide and Schiffrin, *Correspondance*, 156.

15. André Schiffrin, *A Political Education: Coming of Age in Paris and New York* (New York: Melville House, 2007), 28.

16. Letter from Gaston Gallimard to Jacques Schiffrin, November 5, 1940. Schiffrin family archives, personal archives, New York/Correspondence Gallimard.

17. Pierre Assouline, *Gaston Gallimard, un demi-siècle d'édition française* (Paris: Gallimard, 2006), 376.

18. Frank Lestringant, *André Gide, L'Inquiéteur* (Paris: Flammarion, 2012), 912.

19. André Schiffrin, *A Political Education*, 25.

20. Jean-Yves Mollier, *Édition, presse et pouvoir en France au XXème siècle*, (Paris: Fayard, 2008), 139.

21. Mollier, *Édition*, 56.

22. Letter from Jacques Schiffrin to Dimitri Snégaroff, June 21, 1941. "Jacques Schiffrin et les éditions de La Pléiade." *Imprimerie Union*. http://imprimerie-union.org/apollinaire-a-maeght/jacques-schiffrin.

23. Assouline, *Gaston Gallimard*, 378.

24. Pascal Fouché, "L'édition française sous l'occupation, 1940–1944," *Paris: Bibliothèque de littérature française contemporaine de l'Université Paris 7* (1987), 67.

25. Assouline, *Gaston Gallimard*, 383.

26. Assouline, *Gaston Gallimard*, 383.

27. André Schiffrin, *A Political Education*, 28.

28. Letter from Jacques Schiffrin to Dimitri Snégaroff, 3 November 1940: http://imprimerie-union.org/apollinaire-a-maeght/jacques-schiffrin.

29. Fouché, *L'édition française*, 70.

30. Pierre Drieu la Rochelle (1893–1945) was a French writer and literary critic. An active Nazi collaborator, he committed suicide when the war ended.

31. Fouché, *L'édition française*, 71.

32. Fouché, *L'édition française*, 73.

33. Letter from Jacques Schiffrin to Dimitri Snégaroff, December 22, 1940. "Jacques Schiffrin et les éditions de La Pléiade." *Imprimerie Union*. http://imprimerie-union.org/apollinaire-a-maeght/jacques-schiffrin.

34. The infamous *Rafle du Vel d'Hiv* was a roundup and arrest of thousands of Parisian Jews that took place the night of July 16/17, 1942. More than thirteen thousand Jews, including four thousand children, were sent to a large sports stadium, the *Vélodrome d'Hiver*, before being deported to death camps.

35. "Dimitri Snégaroff." *Imprimerie Union*. http://imprimerie-union.org /annees-russes/snegaroff.

36. Letter from Jacques Schiffrin to Dimitri Snégaroff, December 22, 1940. "Jacques Schiffrin et les éditions de La Pléiade." *Imprimerie Union*. http://imprimerie-union.org/apollinaire-a-maeght/jacques -schiffrin.

37. Letter from Jacques Schiffrin to Jean Paulhan, November 9, 1940. Institut mémoire de l'édition contemporaine (IMEC), abbaye d'Ardenne, France. Fonds Paulhan. Correspondence Paulhan-Schiffrin. PLH 197.17.

38. Letter from Jacques Schiffrin to Jean Paulhan, November 9, 1940.

39. André Schiffrin, *A Political Education*, 28–29.

40. Letter from Roger Martin du Gard to Jacques Schiffrin, January 11, 1941. Bibliothèque littéraire Jacques Doucet, Paris. Don Schiffrin. Ms Ms 51187.

41. Letter from Roger Martin du Gard to Jacques Schiffrin, January 11, 1941.

42. Gide and Schiffrin, *Correspondance*, 158–59.

43. Gide and Martin du Gard, *Correspondance*, 227.

44. Gide and Martin du Gard, *Correspondance*, 232.

45. Letter from Roger Martin du Gard to Jacques Schiffrin, February 9, 1941. Bibliothèque littéraire Jacques Doucet, Paris. Don Schiffrin. Ms Ms 51187.

46. Letter from Jacques Schiffrin to Gustavo Gili, February 15, 1941. Schiffrin family archives, personal archives, New York/Correspondence Gili.

47. Gide and Schiffrin, *Correspondance*, 162.

48. Gide and Schiffrin, *Correspondance*, 164.

49. Letter from Jacques Schiffrin to Gustavo Gili. Schiffrin family archives, personal archives, New York/Correspondence Gili.

50. Emmanuelle Loyer, *Paris à New York : intellectuels français et artistes français en exil 1940–1947* (Paris: Fayard, 2007), 37.

51. André Schiffrin, *A Political Education*, 30.

52. Letter from Jacques Schiffrin to Gustavo Gili, February 22, 1941. Schiffrin family archives, personal archives, New York/Correspondence Gili.

53. Letter from Jacques Schiffrin to Gustavo Gili, March 1941. Schiffrin family archives, personal archives, New York/Correspondence Gili.

54. Gide and Schiffrin, *Correspondance*, 164–66.

55. André Schiffrin, *A Political Education*, 31.

56. On Varian Fry, see the conference proceedings of the 1999 Marseille symposium: Jean-Marie Guillon, *Varian Fry: From Refuge to Exile*, vol. 2 (Arles, France: Actes Sud, 2000).

57. Letter from André Gide to Varian Fry, February 1941. Columbia University, Rare Book and Manuscript Library, Varian Fry Papers, Series I: Cataloged Correspondence, Box 1, "André Gide."

58. List of clients of the American Rescue Center. Columbia University, Rare Book and Manuscript Library, Varian Fry Papers, Series I, Cataloged Correspondence, Box 10: "Complete List of Clients of the American Rescue Center."

59. Emergency Rescue Committee report, September 1941. Columbia University, Rare Book and Manuscript Library, Varian Fry Papers, Series I, Cataloged Correspondence, Box 7: "Official Report: The Important Stages of the Committee's Development."

60. Emergency Rescue Committee report, September 1941.

61. Emergency Rescue Committee report, September 1941.

62. Emergency Rescue Committee report, September 1941.

63. Jacques Schiffrin's passport. Schiffrin family archives, personal archives, New York/Administrative Papers.

64. André Schiffrin, *A Political Education*, 34.

65. Letter from Jacques Schiffrin to Gustavo Gili, April 1941. Schiffrin family archives, personal archives, New York/Correspondence Gili.

66. Emergency Rescue Committee report, September 1941.

67. André Schiffrin, *A Political Education*, 34–35.

68. Letter from Jacques Schiffrin to Gustavo Gili, June 16, 1941. Schiffrin family archives, personal archives, New York/Correspondence Gili.

69. van Rysselberghe, *Les Cahiers*, 254.

70. van Rysselberghe, *Les Cahiers*, 68.

71. Catherine was Gide's daughter.

72. Gide and Schiffrin, *Correspondance*, 168.

73. Gide and Schiffrin, *Correspondance*, 169.

74. Lestringant, *André Gide*, 974.

75. Correspondence between Gustavo Gili and Jacques Schiffrin. Schiffrin family archives, personal archives, New York/Correspondence Gili.

76. Letter from Roger Martin du Gard to Jacques Schiffrin, June 12, 1941. Schiffrin family archives, personal archives, New York/Correspondence Martin du Gard.

77. Gide and Schiffrin, *Correspondance*, 170.

78. Letter from Roger Martin du Gard to Jacques Schiffrin, June 26, 1941. Schiffrin family archives, personal archives, New York/Correspondence Martin du Gard.

79. Unless otherwise indicated, the following information and quotes are from the correspondence between Gustavo Gili and Jacques Schiffrin held in the Schiffrin family archives, personal archives, New York/ Correspondence Gili.

80. Letter from Roger Martin du Gard to Jacques Schiffrin, July 4, 1941. Schiffrin family archives, personal archives, New York/Correspondence Martin du Gard.

81. Jacques Schiffrin's passport. Schiffrin family archives, personal archives, New York/Administrative Papers.

82. "Motonave Infanta Beatriz y Ciudad de Sevilla." *Vida Maritima*. Accessed May 20, 2018. https://vidamaritima.com/2007/08/motonave -infanta-beatriz-y-ciudad-de-sevilla/.

83. André Schiffrin, *A Political Education*, 35–36.

84. Julien Green, *Oeuvres complètes*, vol. 4 (Paris: Gallimard, 1976), 603.

85. Letter from Jacques Schiffrin to Gustavo Gili. Schiffrin family archives, personal archives, New York/Correspondence Gili.

86. Victor Brombert, *Les Trains du souvenir: Paris—York—Omaha Beach— Berlin* (Paris: Éditions de Fallois, 2005), 198–216.

87. Claude Lévi-Strauss, *Tristes Tropiques* (Paris: Plon, 1955), 19. This book was published in English under the title *A World on the Wane*.

2. A PUBLISHER IN NEW YORK

1. Several American writers have already considered the question of French artists and intellectuals in exile in New York; for example, Jeffrey Mehlman's *Emigré New York: French Intellectuals in Wartime Manhattan, 1940–1944* (Baltimore, MD: Johns Hopkins University Press, 2000), and Colin Nettelbeck's pioneering work in the field: *Forever French: Exile in the United States, 1939–1945* (Oxford: Berg, 1991).

2. This is the title of Stefan Zweig's autobiography; the original was published in German under the title *Die Welt von Gestern* in Stockholm in 1942.

3. Hannah Arendt, "We Refugees," *The Menorah Journal* 31, no. 1 (1943): 69.

4. Arendt, "We Refugees," 69.

5. Arendt, "We Refugees," 69.

6. Edward Said, *Reflections on Exile and Other Essays* (Cambridge, MA: Harvard University Press, 2002), 173.

7. Said, *Reflections*, 181.

8. Said, *Reflections*, 186.

9. Emmanuelle Loyer, *Paris à New York : intellectuels français et artistes français en exil 1940–1947* (Paris: Fayard, 2007), 65.

10. Letter from Jacques Maritain to Jacques Schiffrin, September 1, 1941. Bibliothèque littéraire Jacques Doucet, Paris. Don Schiffrin. Ms Ms 51186.

11. Julien Green, *Oeuvres complètes*, vol. 4 (Paris: Gallimard, 1976), 603.

12. Green, *Journal*, vol. 4, 629.

13. Svetlana Alexeïeff, interview with the author, Westport, MA, April 29, 2014.

14. Alexeïeff, interview with the author, April 29, 2014.

15. André Gide and Jacques Schiffrin, *Correspondance, 1922–1950* (Paris: Gallimard, 2005), 172.

16. Gide and Schiffrin, *Correspondance*, 174.

17. Letter from Roger Martin du Gard to Jacques Schiffrin, November 5, 1941. Schiffrin family archives, personal archives, New York/Correspondence Martin du Gard.

18. Letter from Jacques Schiffrin to Gustavo Gili. Schiffrin family archives, personal archives, New York/Correspondence Gili.

19. Letter from Gustavo Gili to Jacques Schiffrin, December 31, 1941. Schiffrin family archives, personal archives, New York/Correspondence Gili.

20. Schiffrin family archives, personal archives, New York.

21. Alexeïeff, interview with the author, April 29, 2014.

22. André Schiffrin, *A Political Education: Coming of Age in Paris and New York* (New York: Melville House, 2007), 18.

23. Letter from Jacques Schiffrin to Gustavo Gili, October 8, 1941. Schiffrin family archives, personal archives, New York/Correspondence Gili.

24. Gide and Schiffrin, *Correspondance*, 176.

25. Gide and Schiffrin, *Correspondance*, 176.

26. Gide and Schiffrin, *Correspondance*, 176.

27. Letter from Simone Schiffrin to her sister, Jacqueline, July 17, 1945. Schiffrin family archives, personal archives, New York/Simone Schiffrin papers.

28. "Yacha" was Jacques's nickname within the family.

29. Letter from Simone Schiffrin to her sister, Jacqueline, July 17, 1945.

30. Letter from Simone Schiffrin to her sister, Jacqueline, July 17, 1945.

31. Note from Simone Schiffrin to Jacques Schiffrin. Schiffrin family archives, personal archives, New York/Simone Schiffrin papers.

32. Letter from Simone Schiffrin to her sister, Jacqueline, July 17, 1945.

33. Gide and Schiffrin, *Correspondance*, 177.

34. Gide and Schiffrin, *Correspondance*, 184.

35. Letter from Jacques Schiffrin to Gustavo Gili, October 8, 1941. Schiffrin family archives, personal archives, New York/Correspondence Gili.

36. Loyer, *Paris à New York*, 97.

37. Loyer, *Paris à New York*, 97.

38. Loyer, *Paris à New York*, 97.

39. Loyer, *Paris à New York*, 97.

40. Antoine Bon, *Livres français parus en Amérique de 1940 à 1944* (Rio de Janeiro: n. p., 1944).

41. Gide and Schiffrin, *Correspondance*, 183.

42. Letter from Gaston Gallimard to Jacques Schiffrin, October 31, 1941. Schiffrin family archives, personal archives, New York/Correspondence Gallimard.

43. Gide and Schiffrin, *Correspondance*, 187.

44. Gide and Schiffrin, *Correspondance*, 188.

45. Letter from Jacques Schiffrin to Boris Souvarine, August 2, 1942. Harvard University Library, Boris Souvarine Papers, 1915–1984, Series I: Letters to Boris Souvarine, 1169: Jacques Schiffrin.

46. Colin Nettelbeck, *Forever French, Exile in the United States, 1939–1945* (New York: Berg, 1991), 65.

47. Gide and Schiffrin, *Correspondance*, 189.

48. André Schiffrin, *A Political Education*, 43.

49. The title of the book published in New York by Schiffrin was plural: Les Silences de la mer, for reasons unknown, whereas it was published clandestinely in France by Éditions de Minuit in 1942 as *Le Silence de la mer* (The Silence of the Sea). It was written by Jean Marcel Bruller under the pseudonym "Vercors" and made into a film in 1947.

50. Joseph Kessel (1898–1979) was a French writer and Resistance fighter.

51. André Schiffrin, *A Political Education*, 44.

52. John B. Hench, *Books as Weapons*, (Ithaca, NY: Cornell University Press, 2010).

53. Gide and Schiffrin, *Correspondance*, 190.

54. Gide and Schiffrin, *Correspondance*, 190.

55. Gide and Schiffrin, *Correspondance*, 191.

56. Gide and Schiffrin, *Correspondance*, 194.

57. *"Hénaurme"* is a tribute to Flaubert, who used the expression in his correspondence to express how huge something might be.

58. Gide and Schiffrin, *Correspondance*, 198.

59. Letter from Nadia Boulanger to Jacques Schiffrin, November 17, 1943. Bibliothèque littéraire Jacques Doucet, Paris. Don Schiffrin. Ms Ms 51153.

60. *Cahiers du silence* was a publication of Free France in London.

61. Gide and Schiffrin, *Correspondance*, 200.

62. Denis de Rougemont (1906–1985) was Swiss writer, cultural theorist, and founder of the European Center of Culture in Geneva.

63. André Rouchaud was an associate of Schiffrin's at Jacques Schiffrin & Co.

64. Letter from Jacques Schiffrin to André Breton, February 29, 1944. Bibliothèque littéraire Jacques Doucet, Paris. Fonds André Breton. BRT C Sup 751.

65. Letter from Julien Green to Jacques Schiffrin, May 14, 1942. Bibliothèque littéraire Jacques Doucet, Paris. Don Schiffrin. Ms Ms 51173.

66. Letter from Julien Green to Jacques Schiffrin, July 22, 1942. Bibliothèque littéraire Jacques Doucet, Paris. Don Schiffrin. Ms Ms 51173.

67. Letter from Denis de Rougemont to Jacques Schiffrin, March 7, 1944. Bibliothèque littéraire Jacques Doucet, Paris. Don Schiffrin. Ms Ms 51195.

68. Gide and Schiffrin, *Correspondance*, 218, 238.

69. Gide and Schiffrin, *Correspondance*, 209.

70. Gide and Schiffrin, *Correspondance*, 215.

71. Gide and Schiffrin, *Correspondance*, 228.

72. Gide and Schiffrin, *Correspondance*, 218.

73. Gide and Schiffrin, *Correspondance*, 307.

74. Gide and Schiffrin, *Correspondance*, 201.

75. André Schiffrin, *A Political Education*, 44.

76. Letter from Jacques Schiffrin to Gustavo Gili, October 1941. Schiffrin family archives, personal archives, New York/Correspondence Gili.

77. Alexeïeff, interview with the author, April 29, 2014.

78. Loyer, *Paris à New York*, 68.

79. Letter from Jacques Schiffrin to Henry W. Lanier, February 21, 1949. Yale University Beinecke Rare Book & Manuscript Library, Elizabeth Mayer and Wolfgang Sauerlander Papers, circa 1933–1977, Series II, Wolfgang Sauerlander Correspondence, Box 2, Folder 18: Schiffrin, Jacques, Letters and Memos.

80. On Kurt Wolff, see Kurt Wolff, *Kurt Wolff: A Portrait in Essays and Letters*, trans. Deborah Lucas Schneider (Chicago: University of Chicago Press, 1991), and Laura Fermi, *Illustrious Immigrants: The Intellectual Migration from Europe, 1930–1941* (Chicago: University of Chicago Press, 1968), 276–78.

81. On the close relationship between the Schiffrin and Wolff, see Hendrik Edelman, "Kurt Wolff and Jacques Schiffrin, Two Publishing Giants Start Over in America," in *Immigrant Publishers*, ed. Richard Abel and Gordon Graham (Piscataway, NJ: Transaction, 2009), 185–94.

82. Wolff, *Kurt Wolff*, xxvi.

83. Fermi, *Illustrious Immigrants*, 280.

84. Pantheon's catalog, Random House Archives, New York.

85. The catalog of Jacques Schiffrin & Co. was legally turned over to Pantheon Books on October 29, 1945, for $2,324.07 (Schiffrin Archives).

86. "Bible paper" refers to onion-skin paper.

87. Gide and Schiffrin, *Correspondance*, 243.

88. Letter from Darius Milhaud to Jacques Schiffrin. Bibliothèque littéraire Jacques Doucet, Paris. Don Schiffrin, Paris. Ms Ms 51190.

89. Pantheon's catalog, Random House Archives, New York.

90. Random House Archives, New York.

91. Letter from Jacques Schiffrin to Simon Schiffrin, January 26, 1945. Schiffrin family archives, personal archives, New York.

92. See William McGuire, *Bollingen: An Adventure in Collecting the Past* (Princeton, NJ: Princeton University Press, 1989).

93. Alexeïeff, interview with the author, April 29, 2014.

94. André Schiffrin, *A Political Education*, 51.

95. Correspondence between Jacques Schiffrin and Kurt Wolff. Schiffrin family archives, personal archives, New York.

96. Gide and Schiffrin, *Correspondance*, 305.

97. Schiffrin is undoubtedly referring to the Swedish writer Selma Lagerlöf.
98. Correspondence between Jacques Schiffrin and Wolfgang Sauerlander. Yale University Beinecke Rare Book & Manuscript Library, Elizabeth Mayer and Wolfgang Sauerlander Papers, circa 1933–1977, Series II, Wolfgang Sauerlander Correspondence, Box 2, Folder 18: Schiffrin, Jacques, Letters and Memos.
99. Schiffrin family archives, personal archives, New York/Jacques Oddities.
100. Schiffrin family archives, personal archives, New York/Jacques Oddities.
101. Schiffrin family archives, personal archives, New York/Jacques Oddities.
102. Bibliothèque littéraire Jacques Doucet, Paris. Don Schiffrin. Ms Ms 51217.
103. Bibliothèque littéraire Jacques Doucet, Paris. Don Schiffrin. Ms Ms 51217.
104. Adolfo Bioy Casares (1914–1999) was an Argentine writer, journalist, and translator.
105. Bibliothèque littéraire Jacques Doucet, Paris. Don Schiffrin. Ms Ms 51219.
106. Bibliothèque littéraire Jacques Doucet, Paris. Don Schiffrin. Ms Ms 51219.
107. Letter from Roger Caillois to Jacques Schiffrin, March 20, 1944. Bibliothèque littéraire Jacques Doucet, Paris. Don Schiffrin, Paris. Ms Ms 51155.
108. Bibliothèque littéraire Jacques Doucet, Paris. Don Schiffrin, Paris. Ms Ms 51220.
109. Correspondence between Jacques Schiffrin and the Beauchemin Bookstore (Montreal). Schiffrin family archives, personal archives, New York/Publishing Correspondence.
110. Letter from Jacques Schiffrin to Simon Schiffrin. Schiffrin family archives, personal archives, New York.
111. Correspondence between Jacques Schiffrin and Kurt Wolff. Schiffrin family archives, personal archives, New York.
112. Letter from Jean Bruller (a.k.a. Vercors) to Jacques Schiffrin. Bibliothèque littéraire Jacques Doucet, Paris. Don Schiffrin. Ms Ms 51202.

113. Letter from André Malraux to Jacques Schiffrin, November 30, 1945. Bibliothèque littéraire Jacques Doucet, Paris. Don Schiffrin. Ms Ms 51184.

114. Letter from Jean Pauhan to Jacques Schiffrin, July 21, 1948. Institut mémoire de l'édition contemporaine (IMEC), abbaye d'Ardenne, France. Fonds Paulhan. Correspondance Paulhan–Schiffrin. PLH 197.17.

115. Letter from Jacques Schiffrin to Jean Paulhan, August 9, 1948. Institut mémoire de l'édition contemporaine (IMEC), abbaye d'Ardenne, France. Fonds Paulhan. Correspondance Paulhan–Schiffrin. PLH 197.17.

116. Letter from Jean Paulhan to Jacques Schiffrin, October 12, 1948. Institut mémoire de l'édition contemporaine (IMEC), abbaye d'Ardenne, France. Fonds Paulhan. Correspondance Paulhan–Schiffrin. PLH 197.17.

117. Letter from Jacques Schiffrin to Jean Paulhan, October 19, 1948. Institut mémoire de l'édition contemporaine (IMEC), abbaye d'Ardenne, France. Fonds Paulhan. Correspondance Paulhan–Schiffrin. PLH 197.17.

118. Letter from Robert Aron to Jacques Schiffrin, October 8, 1943. Bibliothèque littéraire Jacques Doucet, Paris. Don Schiffrin. Ms Ms 51143.

119. Letter from Robert Aron to Jacques Schiffrin, December 7, 1943. Bibliothèque littéraire Jacques Doucet, Paris. Don Schiffrin. Ms Ms 51143.

120. Gide and Schiffrin, *Correspondance*, 214.

121. Loyer, *Paris à New York*, 98.

122. Letter from Rachel Bespaloff to Jacques Schiffrin, 1944. Bibliothèque littéraire Jacques Doucet, Paris. Don Schiffrin. Ms Ms 51148.

123. Yale University Beinecke Rare Book & Manuscript Library, Hermann Broch Archive, Series I: Correspondence, Box 12, Folder 350: Jacques Schiffrin.

124. Meyer Schapiro (1904–1996) was one of the most important American art historians.

125. André Schiffrin, *A Political Education*, 50.

126. André Schiffrin, *A Political Education*, 111.

127. André Schiffrin, *A Political Education*, 111.

128. Gide and Schiffrin, *Correspondance*, 226.

3. THE IMPOSSIBLE RETURN

1. André Schiffrin, *A Political Education: Coming of Age in Paris and New York* (New York: Melville House, 2007), 42.

2. Maria van Rysselberghe, *Les Cahiers de la Petite Dame*, vol. 3 (Paris: Gallimard, 1998), 307.

3. Emmanuelle Loyer, *Paris à New York : intellectuels français et artistes français en exil 1940–1947* (Paris: Fayard, 2007), 343–44.

4. André Gide and Jacques Schiffrin, *Correspondance, 1922–1950* (Paris: Gallimard, 2005), 210.

5. Gide and Schiffrin, *Correspondance*, 226.

6. Gide and Schiffrin, *Correspondance*, 233.

7. Gide and Schiffrin, *Correspondance*, 235.

8. Gide and Schiffrin, *Correspondance*, 251.

9. Gide and Schiffrin, *Correspondance*, 260.

10. Gide and Schiffrin, *Correspondance*, 263.

11. Gide and Schiffrin, *Correspondance*, 271.

12. Gide and Schiffrin, *Correspondance*, 276.

13. Gide and Schiffrin, *Correspondance*, 279.

14. Letter from Jacques Schiffrin to Roger Martin du Gard, April 1948. B.N.F. Fonds Roger Martin du Gard. NAF 28190 (119), F. 234–41.

15. Gide and Schiffrin, *Correspondance*, 331.

16. Gide and Schiffrin, *Correspondance*, 287.

17. This comes from the first line of Mallarmé's poem *Brise marine* (*Sea Breeze*), which continues "and I've read all the books."

18. Gide and Schiffrin, *Correspondance*, 340.

19. Gide and Schiffrin, *Correspondance*, 287.

20. Letter from Roger Martin du Gard to Jacques Schiffrin, March 1942. Schiffrin family archives, personal archives, New York/Correspondence Martin du Gard.

21. Letter from Roger Martin du Gard to Jacques Schiffrin, May 1945. Schiffrin family archives, personal archives, New York/Correspondence Martin du Gard.

22. Letter from Roger Martin du Gard to Jacques Schiffrin, January 17, 1947. Schiffrin family archives, personal archives, New York/Correspondence Martin du Gard.

23. Letter from Jacques Schiffrin to Roger Martin du Gard, April 1948. B.N.F. Fonds Roger Martin du Gard. NAF 28190 (119), F. 234–41.

24. Letter from Jacques Schiffrin to Jean Paulhan, January 13, 1947. Institut mémoire de l'édition contemporaine (IMEC), abbaye d'Ardenne, France. Fonds Paulhan. Correspondence Paulhan–Schiffrin. PLH 197.17.

25. Letter from Jacques Schiffrin to Jean Paulhan, January 13, 1947.

26. This is a reference to the title of Stefan Zweig's book *The World of Yesterday*.

27. Alban Cerisier, "Du point de vue de l'éditeur. La *Pléiade* en ses murs," in *La Bibliothèque de la Pléiade, Travail éditorial et valeur littéraire*, ed. Joëlle Gleize and Philippe Roussin (Paris: Éditions des Archives Contemporaines, 2009), 25.

28. Cerisier, "Du point de vue de l'éditeur," 27.

29. Letter from Jean Paulhan to Jacques Schiffrin, April 21, 1944. Institut mémoire de l'édition contemporaine (IMEC), abbaye d'Ardenne, France. Fonds Paulhan. Correspondance Paulhan-Schiffrin. PLH 197.17.

30. Gide and Schiffrin, *Correspondance*, 181.

31. Letter from Raymond Gallimard to Jacques Schiffrin, September 11, 1944. Schiffrin family archives, personal archives, New York/Correspondence Gallimard.

32. Gide and Schiffrin, *Correspondance*, 243.

33. Gide and Schiffrin, *Correspondance*, 246.

34. Letter from Raymond Gallimard to Jacques Schiffrin, April 16, 1945. Schiffrin family archives, personal archives, New York/Correspondence Gallimard.

35. Letter from Raymond Gallimard to Jacques Schiffrin, November 17, 1945. Schiffrin family archives, personal archives, New York/Correspondence Gallimard.

36. Gide and Schiffrin, *Correspondance*, 270.

37. Letter from Raymond Gallimard to Jacques Schiffrin, n.d.. Schiffrin family archives, personal archives, New York/Correspondence Gallimard.

38. Gide and Schiffrin, *Correspondance*, 273.

39. Schiffrin family archives, personal archives, New York.

40. Schiffrin family archives, personal archives, New York.

41. Gide and Schiffrin, *Correspondance*, 277.

42. Gide and Schiffrin, *Correspondance*, 279.

43. Gide and Schiffrin, *Correspondance*, 281.

44. Letter from Jacques Schiffrin to Jean Paulhan, January 13, 1947. Institut mémoire de l'édition contemporaine (IMEC), abbaye d'Ardenne, France. Fonds Paulhan. Correspondence Paulhan-Schiffrin. PLH 197.17.

45. Gide and Schiffrin, *Correspondance*, 330.

46. Gide and Schiffrin, *Correspondance*, 325.

47. Gide and Schiffrin, *Correspondance*, 327.

48. André Gide and Roger Martin du Gard, *Correspondance* (Paris: Gallimard, 1997), 454.

49. Letter from Roger Martin du Gard to Jacques Schiffrin, July 1949. Schiffrin family archives, personal archives, New York/Correspondence Martin du Gard.

50. Letter from Roger Martin du Gard to Jacques Schiffrin, January 17, 1947. Schiffrin family archives, personal archives, New York/Correspondence Martin du Gard.

51. Sartre famously refused to accept the Nobel Prize in Literature in 1964.

52. Emmanuelle Loyer, *Paris à New York : intellectuels français et artistes français en exil 1940–1947* (Paris: Fayard, 2007), 348.

53. Letter from Roger Martin du Gard to Jacques Schiffrin, 1948. Schiffrin family archives, personal archives, New York/Correspondence Martin du Gard.

54. André Schiffrin, *A Political Education: Coming of Age in Paris and New York* (New York: Melville House, 2007), 59.

55. Schiffrin family archives, personal archives, New York/André Files.

56. André Schiffrin, *A Political Education*, 39.

57. André Schiffrin, *A Political Education*, 45.

58. André Schiffrin, *A Political Education*, 46.

59. Gide and Schiffrin, *Correspondance*, 210.

60. Letter from Simone Schiffrin to her sister, Jacqueline, July 17, 1945. Schiffrin family archives, personal archives, New York/Simone Schiffrin Papers.

61. Gide and Schiffrin, *Correspondance*, 235.

62. Schiffrin family archives, personal archives, New York/André Files.

63. Gide and Schiffrin, *Correspondance*, 278.

64. Gide and Schiffrin, *Correspondance*, 302.

65. Gide and Schiffrin, *Correspondance*, 317.

66. Gide and Schiffrin, *Correspondance*, 318.

67. Gide and Schiffrin, *Correspondance*, 318.

68. Gide and Schiffrin, *Correspondance*, 318.

69. Gide and Schiffrin, *Correspondance*, 321–22.

70. Gide and Schiffrin, *Correspondance*, 321–22.

71. André Schiffrin, *A Political Education*, 61.

72. André Schiffrin, *A Political Education*, 62.

73. André Schiffrin, *A Political Education*, 65.

74. André Schiffrin, *A Political Education*, 65.

75. Gide and Schiffrin, *Correspondance*, 326.

76. Gide and Schiffrin, *Correspondance*, 332.

77. Gide and Schiffrin, *Correspondance*, 333.

78. Letter from Roger Martin du Gard to Jacques Schiffrin, July 1949. Schiffrin family archives, personal archives, New York/Correspondence Martin du Gard.

79. Letter from Roger Martin du Gard to Jacques Schiffrin, July 1949.

80. André Schiffrin, *A Political Education*, 77.

81. André Schiffrin, *A Political Education*, 79.

82. Gide and Schiffrin, *Correspondance*, 338.

83. Gide and Schiffrin, *Correspondance*, 298.

84. Gide and Schiffrin, *Correspondance*, 296.

85. Gide and Schiffrin, *Correspondance*, 298.

86. Gide and Schiffrin, *Correspondance*, 300.

87. Gide and Schiffrin, *Correspondance*, 287.

88. Letter from Raymond Gallimard to Jacques Schiffrin, 1945. Schiffrin family archives, personal archives, New York/Correspondence Gallimard.

89. Gide and Schiffrin, *Correspondance*, 325.

90. Gide and Schiffrin, *Correspondance*, 329.

91. Gide and Schiffrin, *Correspondance*, 327.

92. Gide and Martin du Gard, *Correspondance*, 453–54.

93. Letter from Roger Martin du Gard to Jacques Schiffrin, July 4, 1949. Schiffrin family archives, personal archives, New York/Correspondence Martin du Gard.

94. Gide and Schiffrin, *Correspondance*, 329.

95. Gide and Schiffrin, *Correspondance*, 313.

96. Gide and Schiffrin, *Correspondance*, 329.

97. Letter from Roger Martin du Gard to Jacques Schiffrin, July 4, 1949. Schiffrin family archives, personal archives, New York/Correspondence Martin du Gard.

98. Gide and Schiffrin, *Correspondance*, 330.

99. André Schiffrin, *A Political Education*, 59.

100. Gide and Schiffrin, *Correspondance*, 340.

101. André Schiffrin, *A Political Education*, 27.

102. Correspondence between Jacques Schiffrin and Kurt Wolff. Schiffrin family archives, personal archives, New York.

103. Gide and Schiffrin, *Correspondance*, 235.

104. Gide and Schiffrin, *Correspondance*, 300–301.

105. Gide and Schiffrin, *Correspondance*, 339.

106. Gide and Schiffrin, *Correspondance*, 342.

107. André Gide, quoted in Gide and Schiffrin, *Correspondance*, 342.

108. Gide and Schiffrin, *Correspondance*, 340.

109. André Schiffrin, *A Political Education*, 116.

110. Gide and Schiffrin, *Correspondance*, 317.

111. André Schiffrin, *A Political Education*, 123.

112. Letter from Jacques Schiffrin to Roger Martin du Gard, January 17, 1950. B.N.F. Fonds Roger Martin du Gard. NAF 28190 (119), F. 234–41.

113. Svetlana Alexeïeff, interview with the author, Westport, MA, April 29, 2014.

114. Letter from Jacques Schiffrin to Roger Martin du Gard, August 7, 1950. B.N.F. Fonds Roger Martin du Gard. NAF 28190 (119), F. 234–41.

115. Letter from Boris de Schloezer to Jacques Schiffrin, October 1950. Schiffrin family archives, personal archives, New York

116. Letter from Jacques Schiffrin to Raymond Gallimard, October 24, 1950. Schiffrin family archives, personal archives, New York/Correspondence Gallimard.

117. Svetlana Alexeïeff, interview with the author, April 29, 2014.

118. Letter from Raymond Gallimard to Jacques Schiffrin, November 10, 1950. Schiffrin family archives, personal archives, New York/Correspondence Gallimard.

119. Letter from Raymond Gallimard to Jacques Schiffrin, November 10, 1950.

120. Letter from Simone Schiffrin to Boris de Schloezer, 1950. Schiffrin family archives, personal archives, New York.

121. Letter from Simone Schiffrin to Boris de Schloezer, 1950.

122. André Schiffrin stayed with Madame Martin-Chauffier when he visited Paris in the summer of 1949.

123. Letters of condolence. Schiffrin family archives, personal archives, New York.

124. Letters of condolence. Schiffrin family archives, personal archives, New York.

125. Letters of condolence. Schiffrin family archives, personal archives, New York.

126. Julien Green, *Oeuvres complètes*, vol. 4 (Paris: Gallimard, 1976), 1194.

127. Green, *Journal*, 1194.

128. André Gide, *A Political Education*, 1088.

129. Gide and Schiffrin, *Correspondance*, 345.

130. Letters of condolence. Schiffrin family archives, personal archives, New York.

131. Letters of condolence. Schiffrin family archives, personal archives, New York.

132. Letters of condolence. Schiffrin family archives, personal archives, New York.

133. Letter from Lyolene Schiffrin to Simone Schiffrin, 1950. Schiffrin family archives, personal archives, New York.

134. Letter from Simone Schiffrin to Simon Schiffrin, December 10, 1950. Schiffrin family archives, personal archives, New York.

135. Letters of condolence. Schiffrin family archives, personal archives, New York.

136. Simone Schiffrin would continue to live in New York for another fifteen years before dying in a tragic fire.

137. Hermann Broch, obituary for Jacques Schiffrin. Yale University Beinecke Rare Book & Manuscript Library, Hermann Broch Archive, Series II: Writings, Box 55, Folder 1274: Schiffrin, Jacques (Obituary): Drafts, Typescript, Carbon.

138. Kurt Wolff, obituary for Jacques Schiffrin. Schiffrin family archives, personal archives, New York.

139. Administrative papers/Schiffrin family archives, personal archives, New York.

EPILOGUE

1. Mathieu Lindon, "André Schiffrin entre au Pantheon," *Libération*, December 3, 2013.
2. Lindon, "André Schiffrin entre au Pantheon."
3. "1931, la première *Pléiade*," *Le Monde*, December 1, 1996.

ARCHIVES CONSULTED

HANDWRITTEN SOURCES

France

Bibliothèque littéraire Jacques Doucet, Paris

ANDRÉ SCHIFFRIN DONATION (*DON SCHIFFRIN*)
Ms Ms 51129—Ms Ms 51209; Ms Ms 51212—Ms Ms 51228
Ms Ms 51129—Ms Ms 51140; manuscripts from other authors

MANUSCRIPTS RECEIVED AND EDITED
BY JACQUES SCHIFFRIN
André Gide
Joseph Kessel
Antoine de Saint-Exupéry
Vercors (Jean Bruller)

TRANSLATION WORK ON *LA MORT D'IVAN ILITCH*, TOLSTOY
Ms Ms 51141—Ms Ms 51209; Ms Ms 51212—Ms Ms 51228; correspondence
Ms Ms 51141—Ms Ms 51209; correspondence received by Jacques Schiffrin

PERSONAL CORRESPONDENTS WITH JACQUES SCHIFFRIN
Robert Aron
Rachel Bespaloff
Nadia Boulanger
Hermann Broch
Roger Caillois

Albert Camus
André David
Gaston Doumergue
André Gide
Julien Green
André Malraux
Jacques Maritain
Roger Martin du Gard
Darius Milhaud
Denis de Rougemont
Philippe Soupault
Vercors
Jean Wahl

MS MS 51212—MS MS 51228; EDITORIAL
CORRESPONDENCE
Between Jacques Schiffrin and:
Americ. Edit.
Malcolm Cowley
Emecé Editores
Gallimard
André Gide
Carlos Hirsch
Kenyon Review
Alfred Knopf
Boris de Schloezer

BNF: Bibliothèque nationale de France, Paris

Fonds Roger Martin du Gard: NAF 28190
Lettres Jacques Schiffrin—Roger Martin du Gard, NAF 28190 (119),
    F. 234–241

Institut Mémoires de l'édition contemporaine (IMEC), Abbaye d'Ardenne

Fonds Paulhan: PLH
Correspondance croisée Paulhan–Schiffrin: PLH 197, 197–17

United States

Schiffrin Archives, New York

In André and Leina Schiffrin's apartment on the Upper West Side, numerous important documents regarding Jacques Schiffrin's life have been kept. Some of these archives can also be consulted at the *Bibliothèque littéraire Jacques Doucet.*

The Schiffrin family was extremely kind in allowing me to work with these archives, some of which have never been published. They are divided into various files:

Jacques
Pantheon
Jacques Oddities
Jacques Condolences of Death
Jacques, Children's Book . . .
From Simone Things
André, Letters from Parents
Correspondence Gili

These rich and diverse family archives, including items ranging from birth certificates to correspondence between Kurt Wolff and Jacques Schiffrin, will most likely soon be sent to various archives in both France and the United States. They also contain many photographs of Jacques Schiffrin and his close family and friends.

Anya Schiffrin, one of André and Leina Schiffrin's daughters, invited me to her home to consult certain archives relating to Jacques Schiffrin's life in Baku. She had traveled to Azerbaijan with her father to carry our research on her family's origins. Items in these archives, often written in Russian, make it possible to better understand Jacques Schiffrin's early years.

Columbia University, Rare Book & Manuscript Library, New York, New York

VARIAN FRY PAPERS [CA. 1940]–1967
Series I: Cataloged Correspondence, Volume 1
Box 1
André Gide
Series IV: Subject Files
Box 7
Centre Americain de Secours Adminstrative Reports (1 of 2)
Centre Americain de Secours Adminstrative Reports (2 of 2)
Box 10
Refugees, Lists of Endangered, 1941
Series VII: Printed Material
Box 18
Refugees, Intellectuals, Arrival in the U.S.
Publishers Weekly: Reference Files, 1909–2007
Series I: Reference Files 1909–2007
Box 52
Pantheon Books, Inc., 1942–2005 (two folders)
Pantheon Books Records, 1944–1968
Series II: Alphabetical Files
Box 2
Hermann Broch
Box 16
Henri Peyre
Box 21
Albert Skira
Box 26
Catalogues

Yale University, Beinecke Rare Book & Manuscript Library, New Haven, Connecticut

ELIZABETH MAYER AND WOLFGANG SAUERLANDER PAPERS,
CIRCA 1933–1977
Series II: Wolfgang Sauerlander Correspondence
Box 2, Folder 18: Schiffrin, Jacques, Letters and Memos

HERMANN BROCH ARCHIVE
Series I: Correspondence
Box 9, Folder 272: Pantheon Books
Box 12, Folder 350: Jacques Schiffrin
Box 15, Folder 442: Kurt and Helen Wolff
Series II: Writings
Box 55, Folder 1274: Schiffrin, Jacques (Obituary): Drafts, Typescript, Carbon

Kurt Wolff's archives are also available to be consulted at Yale University. Unfortunately, they do not cover the period of the Second World War. See: Kurt Wolff Archives, 1907–1938, YCGL MSS 3.

Harvard University Library, Cambridge, Massachusetts

SOUVARINE, BORIS. BORIS SOUVARINE PAPERS, 1915–1984
Series I: Letters to Boris Souvarine
File number 1169, Schiffrin, Jacques

Random House, New York, New York

The Random House Group, which owns Pantheon Books, has some archives relating to the history of the publishing house founded in New York during World War II by Kurt Wolff, where Jacques Schiffrin worked early in the press's history. Altie Karper, managing editor at Random House, was kind enough to place some of these documents at my disposal. These are mainly contracts between Pantheon and its authors, as well as various catalogs of the publishing house, year by year, during the war.

DIGITAL SOURCES

Imprimerie Union (Union Printing Press)
Correspondence Jacques Schiffrin–Dimitri Snégaroff (February 1940 to December 1940): http://imprimerie-union.org/apollinaire-a-maeght /jacques-schiffrin.

Interviews

Interviews with Svetlana Alexeïeff-Rockwell, April 29, 2014, Westport, Massachusetts.

Numerous interviews with Anya and Leina Schiffrin on the history of their family, New York, New York, primarily between January and May, 2014.

BIBLIOGRAPHY

Ackermann, Bruno. *Denis de Rougemont, une biographie intellectuelle.* Geneva: Labor et Fides, 1996.

Adorno, Theodor W. *Minima Moralia, Réflexions sur la vie mutilée.* Paris: Payot, 2003.

Alexandre-Garnier, Corinne, and Isabelle Keller-Privat, eds. *Migrations, exils, errances et écritures.* Paris: Presses universitaires de Paris Nanterre, 2012.

Arendt, Hannah. *The Jew as Pariah: Jewish Identity and Politics in the Modern Age.* New York: Grove, 1978.

Assouline, Pierre. *Gaston Gallimard, un demi-siècle d'édition française.* Paris: Folio, 2006.

Backouche, Isabelle, ed. "Figures de l'exil." Special issue. *Genèses, Sciences sociales et histoire,* no. 38 (2000).

Bailyn, Bernard, and Donald Fleming. *The Intellectual Migration: Europe and America, 1930–1960.* Cambridge, MA: Harvard University Press, 1969.

Barré, Jean-Luc. *Jacques et Raïssa Maritain, Les Mendiants du ciel.* Paris: Tempus Perrin, 2012.

Baudelaire, Charles. *Oeuvres complètes.* Paris: Gallimard, 1975–1976.

Beaupré, Nicolas. *Les Grandes Guerres (1914–1945).* Paris: Belin, 2012.

Béhar, Henri. *André Breton, le grand indésirable.* Paris: Calmann-Levy, 1990.

Bellay, Joachim du. *Les Regrets.* Paris: Le Livre de Poche, 2002.

Bernanos, Georges. *Correspondance.* Vol. 2, *1934–1948.* Paris: Plon, 1971.

Bishop, Thomas, and Christine Fauré. *L'Amérique des Français.* Paris: Bourin, 1992.

Bon, Antoine. *Livres français parus en Amérique.* Rio de Janeiro: n.p., 1944.

Brombert, Victor. *Les Trains du souvenir: Paris–New York–Omaha Beach–Berlin.* Paris: Bernard de Fallois, 2005.

Burrin, Philippe. *La France à l'heure allemande*. Paris: Seuil, 1995.

Caillois, Roger. *Circonstancielles (1940–1945)*. Paris: Gallimard, 1946.

Cariguel, Olivier, and Olivier Corpet. *Panorama des revues littéraires sous l'occupation : Juillet 1940, Août 1944*. Caen: IMEC, 2007.

Chassaigne, Philippe, and Jean Marc Largeaud, eds. *Villes en guerre*. Paris: Armand Colin, 2004.

Chartier Roger, and Henri-Jean Martin. *Histoire de l'édition française*. 4 vols. Paris: Fayard, 1989–1991.

Clair, Jean, and Robert Kopp. *De la mélancolie, les Entretiens de la fondation des Treilles*. Paris: Gallimard, 2007.

Cohen-Solal, Annie. *Un jour ils auront des peintres. L'avènement des peintres américains, Paris 1867–New York 1948*. Paris: Gallimard, 2000.

Collomp, Catherine, and Mario Menendez, eds. *Exilés et réfugiés politiques aux Etats-Unis, 1789–2000*. Paris: CNRS, 2003.

Conan, Eric, and Henry Rousso. *Vichy, un passé qui ne passe pas*. Paris: Fayard, 1994.

Corcy, Stéphanie. *La vie culturelle sous l'occupation*. Paris: Perrin, 2005.

Dandrey, Patrick. *Anthologie de l'humeur noire*. Paris: Gallimard, 2005.

Darnton, Robert. *The Case for Books: Past, Present, and Future*. New York: PublicAffairs, 2009.

Darnton, Robert. *Gens de lettres, gens du livre*. Paris: Odile Jacob, 1992.

Dosse, François. *Les hommes de l'ombre, Portraits d'éditeurs*. Paris: Perrin, 2014.

Dostoïevski, Fédor. *L'Idiot*. Paris: Gallimard, 1953.

Duranton-Cabrol, Anne-Marie. *Alvin Johnson et Varian Fry. Au secours des savants et artistes européens*. Paris: Michel Houdiard Éditeur, 2002.

Edelman, Hendrik. "Kurt Wolff and Jacques Schiffrin, Two Publishing Giants Start Over in America." In *Immigrant Publishers*, edited by Richard Abel and Gordon Graham, 185–96. New Brunswick, NJ: Transaction, 2009.

"Exils . . ." *Revue d'histoire moderne et contemporaine* 46, no. 2 (April–June 1999), 245–310.

Fauchere, Serge, ed. *Paris–New York, Échanges littéraires au XXème siècle*. Paris: Bibliothèque publique d'information, Centre national d'art et de culture Georges Pompidou, 1977.

Fermi, Laura. *Illustrious Immigrants: The Intellectual Migration from Europe, 1930–1941*. Chicago: Chicago University Press, 1968.

Flaubert, Gustave. *L'Éducation sentimentale.* Paris: Gallimard, 2005.

Fouché, Pascal. *L'Édition française sous l'occupation, 1940–1944.* 2 vols. Paris: Bibliothèque de littérature française contemporaine de l'Université Paris 7 (1987).

Frank, Robert, ed. *Les États-Unis et les réfugiés politiques européens, des années 1930 aux années 1950.* Special issue. *Matériaux pour l'histoire de notre temps* 60, Octobre–décembre. 2000.

Fritsch-Estrangin, Guy. *New York entre de Gaulle et Pétain, Les Français aux États-Unis de 1940–1946.* Paris: La Table Ronde, 1969.

Fry, Varian. *Surrender on Demand.* New York: Johnson, 1945.

Gide, André. *Journal.* Volume 2, *1926–1950.* Paris: Gallimard, 1997.

Gide, André, and Dorothy Bussy. *Correspondance: janvier 1937, janvier 1951.* Paris: Gallimard, 1982.

Gide, André, and Edmond Jaloux. *Correspondance.* Lyon: Presses universitaires de Lyon, 2005.

Gide, André, and Roger Martin du Gard. *Correspondance.* Paris : Gallimard, 1968.

Gide, André, and Jean Paulhan. *Correspondance, 1918–1951.* Paris : Gallimard, 1998.

Gide, André, and Jacques Schiffrin. *Correspondance, 1922–1950.* Paris : Gallimard, 2005.

——. "Mon ami Schiffrin, André Gide et la Pléiade." *La Lettre de la Pléiade* 2 (Fall 1999), 3.

Gleize, Joëlle, and Philippe Roussin, eds. *La Bibliothèque de la Pléiade, Travail éditorial et valeur littéraire.* Paris: Éditions des Archives Contemporaines, 2009.

Green, Julien. *La fin d'un monde, Juin 1940.* Paris: Éditions du Seuil, 1992.

——. *Journal.* In *Oeuvres complètes,* vol. 4. Paris, Fayard, 1976.

Guggenheim, Peggy. *Out of This Century: Confessions of an Art Addict.* New York: André Deutsch, 1979.

Guillon, Jean-Marie. *Varian Fry, du refuge . . . à l'exil.* 2 vols. Arles: Actes Sud, 2000.

Hebey, Pierre. *La NRF des années sombres.* Paris: Gallimard, 1992.

Hench, John B. *Books as Weapons: Propaganda, Publishing, and the Battle for Global Markets in the Era of World War II.* Ithaca, NY: Cornell University Press, 2010.

Homère. *L'Odyssée*. Paris: Fayard, 1999.

Jablonka, Ivan. *Histoire des grands-parents que je n'ai pas eus : Une enquête*. Paris: Seuil, 2012.

Jankélévitch, Vladimir. *L'irréversible et la nostalgie*. Paris: Flammarion, 2011.

Jay, Martin. *Permanent Exiles: Essays on the Intellectual Migration from Germany to America*. New York: Columbia University Press, 1985.

Jeanpierre, Laurent. *Des hommes entre plusieurs mondes. Étude sur une situation d'exil. Intellectuels français réfugiés aux États-Unis pendant la Deuxième guerre mondiale*. PhD Diss. EHESS. 2 vols. Paris, 2004.

Kaplan, Alice, and Philippe Roussin. "A Changing Idea of Literature: The Bibliothèque de la Pléiade." *Yale French Studies* 89 (1996): 237–62.

Kent, Donald Peterson, *The Refugee Intellectual: The Americanization of the Immigrants of 1933–1941*. New York: Columbia University Press, 1953.

Lapaque, Sébastien. *Sous le soleil de l'exil, Georges Bernanos au Brésil, 1938–1945*. Paris: Grasset, 2003.

Lemire, Vincent. *Jérusalem, 1900 : La ville sainte à l'âge des possibles*. Paris: Armand Colin, 2013.

Lestringant, Frank. *Andre Gide l'inquiéteur*. Vol. 2, *Le sel de la terre ou l'inquiétude assumée 1919–1951*. Paris: Flammarion, 2012.

Lévi-Strauss, Claude. *Tristes tropiques*. Paris: Plon, 1955.

Loyer, Emmanuelle. *Paris à New York, Intellectuels et artistes français en exil, 1940–1947*. Paris: Grasset & Fasquelle, 2005.

Maritain, Jacques. *À travers le désastre*. New York: Éditions de la Maison française, 1941.

——. *Messages, 1941–44*. New York: French & European Publications, 1945.

Marrus, Michael Robert, and Robert O. Paxton. *Vichy France and the Jews*, New York: Basic Books, 1981.

Martin du Gard, Roger. *Journal*. Paris: Gallimard, 1993.

Masanet, Phillipe. *Paris à New York. Intellectuels et artistes français réfugiés à New York, 1940–1946*. Master's thesis. Paris: Université de Paris 1, 1989.

Mazower, Mark. *Dark Continent: Europe's Twentieth Century*. New York: Vintage, 2000.

McGuire, William. *Bollingen: An Adventure in Collecting the Past*. Princeton, NJ: Princeton University Press, 1989.

Mehlman, Jeffrey. *Emigré New York: French Intellectuals in Wartime Manhattan, 1940–1944*. Baltimore, MD: Johns Hopkins University Press, 2000.

Modiano, Patrick. *Dora Bruder*. Paris: Gallimard, 1997.

Mollier, Jean-Yves. *Edition, presse et pouvoir en France au XXème siècle*. Paris: Fayard, 2008.

Nettelbeck, Colin. *Forever French, Exile in the United States, 1939–1945*. New York: Berg, 1991.

Panné, Jean-Louis. *Boris Souvarine, le premier désenchanté du communisme*. Paris: Robert Laffont, 1993.

Paris–New York. Paris: Centre Georges-Pompidou / Gallimard, 1991.

Paxton, Robert O. *Vichy France: Old Guard and New Order, 1940–1944*. New York: Columbia University Press, 1972.

Paxton, Robert O., Olivier Corpet, and Claire Paulhan, eds. *Archives de la vie littéraire sous l'occupation: À travers le désastre*. Paris: Tallandier, 2011.

Perec, Georges. *La Disparition*. Paris: Les Lettres nouvelles, 1969.

——. *Récits d'Ellis Island : Histoires d'errance et d'espoir*. Paris: P.O.L., 1994.

Robert, Valérie. *Partir ou rester? Les intellectuels allemands devant l'exil, 1933–1939*. Paris: Presses de la Sorbonne nouvelle, 2001.

Rougemont, Denis de. *Journal d'une époque, 1926–1946*. Paris: Gallimard, 1968.

——. *La Part du diable*. New York: Brentano's, 1942.

Rysselberghe, Maria van. *Cahiers de la Petite Dame*. 4 vols. Paris: Gallimard, 1973–77.

Said, Edward. *Reflections on Exile and Other Essays*. Cambridge, MA: Harvard University Press, 2002.

Saint-Exupéry, Antoine de. *Écrits de Guerre, 1939–1944*. Paris: Gallimard, 1994.

Sapiro, Gisèle. *La guerre des écrivains, 1940–1953*. Paris: Fayard, 1999.

Sayad, Abdelamalek. *La Double absence, Des Illusions de l'émigré aux souffrances de l'immigré*. Paris: Seuil, 1999.

Schiffrin, André. *L'Édition sans éditeurs*. Paris: La Fabrique Éditions, 1999.

——. *A Political Education: Coming of Age in Paris and New York*. New York: Melville House, 2007.

Tebbel, John. *A History of Book Publishing in the United States*. 4 vols. New York: R. R. Bowker, 1972–81.

Tumarkin Goodman, Susan, and Kenneth E. Silver. *Chagall: Love, War, and Exile*. New Haven, CT: Yale University Press, 2013.

Weil, François. *Les Franco-Américains, 1960–1980*. Paris: Bélin, 1989.

——. *New York*. Paris, 2001.

Wolff, Kurt, and Michael Ermarth. *Kurt Wolff: A Portrait in Essays and Letters*. Chicago: University of Chicago Press, 1991.

Zweig, Stefan. *Le Monde d'hier, souvenirs d'un Européen*. Paris: Belfond, 1982.

Filmography

Curtiz, Michael, dir. *Casablanca*. Burbank, CA: Warner Brothers–Frist National Pictures, 1942.

Dassin, Jules, dir. *The Naked City*. Hollywood, CA: Mark Hellinger Productions, 1948.

Hawks, Howard, dir. *To Have and Have Not*. Burbank, CA: Warner Brothers, 1944.

Tourneur, Jacques, dir. *Cat People*. New York: RKO Radio Pictures, 1942.

INDEX